SCOTTISH REPRINTS

THOUGHTS ON THE PROPOSED CHANGE OF CURRENCY

&

TWO LETTERS ON SCOTTISH AFFAIRS

SIR WALTER SCOTT

THOUGHTS
ON THE PROPOSED
CHANGE OF CURRENCY

&

JOHN WILSON CROKER

TWO LETTERS
ON SCOTTISH AFFAIRS

with introduction by

DAVID SIMPSON &
ALASTAIR WOOD

IRISH UNIVERSITY PRESS
Shannon   Ireland
1972

This volume contains a complete and unabridged photolithographic facsimile of the first pamphlet edition of [Sir Walter Scott's] *Thoughts on the Proposed Change of Currency, and other late Alterations, as they affect, or are intended to affect, the Kingdom of Scotland, with A Second Letter . . . from Malachi Malagrowther, Esq., . . .* and *A Third Letter . . . from Malachi Malagrowther, Esq., ...* Edinburgh (Blackwood) 1826, and [John Wilson Croker's] *Two Letters on Scottish Affairs . . . ,* London (Murray) and Edinburgh (Oliver & Boyd) 1826. The copies here reproduced are in the Scott Collection, Stirling University Library.

ISBN 0 7165 0306 9

Irish University Press Shannon Ireland
T. M. MacGlinchey Publisher

PRINTED IN THE REPUBLIC OF IRELAND
BY ROBERT HOGG PRINTER TO IRISH
UNIVERSITY PRESS

CONTENTS

INTRODUCTION

In the late eighteenth and early nineteenth centuries Scotland possessed a financial system more efficient than that of her larger and richer neighbour, England. Evidence for this is to be found in the letters of Lord Liverpool, Prime Minister at the time of the crisis of 1825—6, and in reports of Committees of the House of Lords and of the Bank of England.

Important differences in the financial systems of the two countries can be traced to an Act of 1708, which effectively gave a monopoly of large-scale banking in England to the Bank of England. No other banking company with more than six partners had the right to issue notes, and since the Bank of England made no attempt to open branches outside London, but was content to take its profit by acting as banker to the Government, this meant that the English provinces were served by a proliferation of some 800 small banking companies. Having little capital, these small banks made advances by simply issuing notes, with slight regard to their ability to retire them when presented. It was scarcely surprising therefore that in a normal year, some 2 per cent of the banks would fail, a proportion which rose to 10 per cent in the years 1825—6.

In Scotland, on the other hand, the number of bank failures had been small in the century prior to 1825, with none in the period 1816—25. Although there were a number of small banking companies left in Scotland, the scene was dominated by three large joint-stock banking companies, each with hundreds of partners, and an extensive network of branches and agencies throughout the country. A tendency to over-issue was constrained by the system according to which the Scottish banks exchanged each others' notes. Any bank which did overissue quickly found its notes returned to it.

The controversy which inspired Scott's inter-vention touched upon another difference between the banking systems of Scotland and England. In England, coin was the principal medium of circulation, while in Scotland bank-notes were the common currency. So long-standing was this distinction that in England there was a widespread distrust of bank-notes, whereas in Scotland attempts by government to suppress the issue of smaller notes aroused popular resentment.

The proposal to suppress the issue of notes below the value of £5 was contained in the banking legislation of 1826, which was the direct result of the financial crisis which began in the autumn of 1825 and continued into the following summer. The origins of that crisis are to be found in a wave of speculative loans and investments in South American mining ventures, which collapsed as quickly as their Australian counterparts today, together with the reckless promotion of companies at home. Of 624 new companies which arose in England in 1824 and 1825, only 127 still existed two years later.

The response of the Government to this crisis was to introduce legislation containing three main provisions: to limit the monopoly of the Bank of England to within a radius of 65 miles from London; to facilitate the opening of branches by the Bank of England outside London; and to forbid the issue of bank-notes under the value of £5 throughout the United Kingdom.

The purpose of the first two provisions was to replace the small English country banks with the larger type of joint-stock banking companies which had developed so successfully in Scotland. While it was reasonable to hold the imprudence of the English country banks largely responsible for the collapse of more than seventy of their number, (compared to Scotland, where there were only two or three bank failures—and not one among the older or fully developed joint-stock banks), there was no justification for thinking that there had been an overissue of small notes. The consequence of extending this prohibition to Scotland, where notes below the value of £5 made up the greater part of the currency in circulation, would of course have been disastrous. The inevitable result would have been a fall in prices, accompanied by a prolonged depression.

In his Journal for 17 February 1826, Scott noted his concern with the question of currency reform. "I am horribly tempted to interfere in this business of altering the system of Banks in Scotland; and yet I know that if I can attract any notice, I will offend my English friends without propitating one man in Scotland." Scott's personal circumstances in February 1826 might have made it unlikely that he would air his views in public, for he had just become spectacularly bankrupt. The financial crisis of 1825—6 had brought into question the credit of many long-established business houses. In a chain reaction of bankruptcies among publishers, Scott became liable for the debts of James Ballantyne's printing and publishing business, of which he was the unpublicised major partner, and for discounted bills, which he had endorsed, of Archibald Constable and Company and Hurst Robinson and Company. Scott's entire liability amounted to more than £104,000.

Scott's motives in writing his Letters on the Currency must have been complex. In the descriptions of national financial mismanagement, we can sense some of his frustration and outrage at his own present position. He was, in some respects, expressing views acceptable to the

Edinburgh banks, for their freedom of business would be severely curtailed by the proposed legislation against bank-notes; they later bespoke five hundred copies of the first pamphlet edition of Scott's First Letter, and they were proving amenable to his own views as to the way in which his debts might be repaid.

But the fundamental emotion Scott is asserting in these Letters is that of national pride. He had been beggared by the failure of an English company to meet its obligations, and foresaw the prospect of Scotland itself being beggared by legislation which, however necessary to remedy the financial affairs of the English and Irish local banks, was irrelevant to conditions north of the Border. His Journal note for 18 February is revealing: "I set about Malachi Malagrowther's Letter on the late disposition to change everything in Scotland to an English model, but without resolving about the publication. They do treat us very provokingly." Equally significant is a remark, in a letter to his eldest son in March 1826: ". . . I think the Ministers have for ten or twelve years been pursuing a system highly insulting towards Scotland and this sudden and violent change of currency will produce the greatest mischief."

Malachi Malagrowther's three Letters show this divided focus. The immediate argument was the utter inadvisability of the measure

proposed, and this is demonstrated in terms of
the "evident utility" to the people of Scotland
of their paper currency. Scott had an over-
whelming economic case on his side. The case is
largely understated, but Scott may shrewdly
have recognised that his attack, with its amusing
anecdotes, literary allusions, and emotional
chauvinism would have far more political appeal
than any amount of dry economic agrument.

Scott touches on nearly all of the practical
advantages of having a paper currency which
would be apparent to any intelligent Scottish
observer of that time. It had facilitated the rapid
progress of Scottish industry and agriculture
in the previous half-century, and in particular
had made available banking services and places
of safe deposit to communities in the remoter
areas, and provided an easier means of transmission of money in a sparsely populated country.

He also deals with some of the prejudices
against the paper currency which were popular
in certain ill-informed circles in England, and
which are clearly portrayed in Croker's letters.
It must be remembered that a paper currency
was regarded in England as only a temporary
expedient in time of war, and inherently inferior
to a metallic currency.

The popular prejudices against the Scottish
paper currency fall into three categories. First,
there is the objection that it is liable to overissue.

But, as Scott points out, this is easily refuted by the historical evidence that in England, where a metallic currency prevailed, bank failures were much more common. One would expect that a paper currency would be liable to fewer of the vicissitudes of expansion and contraction, and this was indeed what happened. During the wave of bank failures in England in 1825—6, the Prime Minister, Lord Liverpool, observed that Scotland appeared to be "immune from the virus". Significantly, there was a considerable circulation of Scottish bank-notes in the North of England, where they enjoyed an acceptability which was not accorded to the notes of the English country banks.

Secondly, forgery had been advanced as an argument against a paper currency, and this was indeed one of the reasons behind the Government's desire to suppress the smaller notes. That so many English forgers were hanged was not likely to reconcile Scottish public opinion to the intrusion of English practices into Scottish administration: that so many were convicted could be attributed to the ridiculous ease with which the Bank of England £1 note could be forged. The Scottish banks, whose notes were more difficult to counterfeit, had little trouble.

Thirdly, it was alleged that it was profitable for the banks to issue their own notes. This was certainly true, but if it had not been profitable to do so it is unlikely that the banks would have provided their services in the remoter parts of the country.

Scott is on weaker ground in arguing that the greater strength of the Scottish banks lay in their capital being secured by land. Land is not an asset which can always be realised at short notice, and therefore does not necessarily provide good security for a bank. Undoubtedly the most remarkable aspect of Scott's argument is his apparent acceptance of the popular English prejudice that a paper currency is inferior to a metallic standard. He defends its existence rather apologetically; Scotland, being a poorer country than England, could not "afford" a metallic currency. In having a paper currency Scotland was, in fact, ahead of England, and no less an authority than Ricardo had advocated the issue of small paper notes "for all the country districts" of England.

Scott's real concern, however, is not economic, but political. His language in his Three Letters is charged with emotion, with appeals to national Scottish pride to assert itself, and with remembrances of what had been done, and what had counted in the past. In this appeal to his readers, Scott was not a perfervid nationalist. His novels had, of course, admitted the emotive appeal of Jacobitism to the young and romantic, but had

always come down firmly on the side of moderation and the Hanoverian future. He was indeed
the loyalest of Tories, and George IV's visit to
Edinburgh in 1822, which Scott had largely
stage-managed, had been regarded as an affirma-
tion of the security and permanence of Scotland's
role in the United Kingdom. Even in appealing
to national sentiment, he did not adopt the
standpoint of a nationalist. His charge against
England (11. 76) was that of unauthorised
encroachment and political disrespect: "There
has been in England a gradual and progressive
system of assuming the management of affairs
entirely and exclusively proper to Scotland, as
if we were totally unworthy of having the management of our own concerns." Established practices
were altered by Commissions unfamiliar with the
Scottish system; old positions were abolished or
amalgamated, without reference to their holders
or the needs of society, and in every respect a
kingdom was being downgraded to a mere northern
county. Above all, Scott sensed a desire to
centralise all decision-making in London, at
maximum convenience to the administrators,
and at maximum inconvenience to everyone else.
The language of his protest (11. 77) has been often
echoed: "We could not be intrusted with the
charge of erecting our own kirks, (churches in
the Highlands,) or of making our roads and bridges
in the same wild districts, but these labours must

be conducted under the tender care of men who knew nothing of our country, its wants and its capabilities, but who, nevertheless, sitting in their office in London, were to decide, without appeal, upon the conduct of the roads in Lochaber!"

In adopting the pseudonym of Malachi Malagrowther, for his Letters on the Currency, Scott was aware of a distinguished literary precedent. In 1724, Jonathan Swift had assumed the mask of M.B., a linen-draper, and in his *Drapier's Letters* persuaded the Irish to oppose a scheme, promoted by an English ironmonger named Wood, to coin base copper pence and half-pence for circulation in Ireland. Swift's letters appealed to the spirit of Irish nationalism, and public opinion triumphed over the dictates of a foreign authority.

Scott loved to adopt facetious masks, as when several of his novels were first published as "collected and arranged by Jedediah Cleishbotham, Schoolmaster and Parish-Clerk of Gandercleugh". His persona on the present occasion was that of a decayed descendant of one of his own fictional characters, Sir Mungo Malagrowther, the crabbed and backbiting old courtier in *The Fortunes of Nigel*. Unlike Swift, who sustained his argument in language suited to his supposed narrator, Scott did not maintain Malagrowther's caustic humour, and there are relatively few passages in the tone of the fictional character. An exception, however, is the opening of the Third Letter, where the portrait of Malagrowther, declaiming his pamphlets in his narrow room (III. 5) is a reminder of Scott's powers as an imaginative, rather than a political or economic writer.

Despite the care given to revision and re-writing, Scott's Three Letters are powerful rather than memorable. The vocabulary is frequently technical, and the sentences complex, but the argument is emotional rather than logical. Scott did not plan the sequence as a rationally developed argument, but rather added another instalment whenever any further point of great importance occurred to him. This is admitted in Scott's Journal entry for 6 March: "Finished 3rd *Malachi*, which I don't much like. It respects the difficulty of finding gold to replace the paper circulation. Now this should have been considered first. The admitting that the measure may be imposed is yielding up the question, and *Malachi* is like a Commandant who should begin to fire from interior defences before his outworks were carried." The Letters, however, had their desired effect and there can be few economic pamphlets which are enlivened by so many literary allusions, or in which the reader is expected to revel in a parody of a contemporary poet, as when Scott enjoys himself at Wordsworth's expense (II. 10).

The copies here reproduced are those of the first pamphlet edition of Scott's three Letters of Malachi Malagrowther, and Croker's two Letters of E. B. Waverley. The pamphlets have been bound up into one volume, and are now in the Scott Collection of the Stirling University Library.

Even though the newspaper and the various pamphlet editions of Malachi Malagrowther's Letters appeared within a few days of each other, they do not represent a simple process of textual transmission by reprint, for Scott indulged himself in an extensive course of revision and addition to his text.

Malachi Malagrowther's Letters first appeared in three consecutive issues of the *Edinburgh Weekly Journal*. This influential periodical had been owned, since March 1817, by a partnership of the Ballantynes and Scott himself. The newspaper usually provided a reasonably comprehensive coverage, often by synopsis, of local, national and foreign news, though, as Scott wrily acknowledged in the opening paragraph of his Third Letter (III. 3), his contributions. had managed to crowd out almost all of the usual items.

> I have trodden on the toes of your Domestic Intelligence, and pushed up to the wall even your Political Debates, until you have almost lost your honoured title of the EDINBURGH JOURNAL in that of MALACHI'S CHRONICLE.

As Scott's Letters were an immediate sensation, they were reprinted almost at once in pamphlet form, by James Ballantyne and Company, for William Blackwood of Edinburgh. The first edition of the new First Letter sold out within two days, and further editions of each pamphlet were advertised within days of the first being published. Scott, however, revised his text with an almost obsessive care, and we can see how his rewriting was designed to strengthen his argument, or to make Malachi's rhetoric the more persuasive.

The First Letter was written on 18 and 19 February, and printed in the *Edinburgh Weekly Journal*, 22 February 1826, pp. 60—2. Its first pamphlet edition was advertised as being published on 1 March, with the second edition a week later; a fourth pamphlet edition had been published by 5 April 1826.

Scott records in his Journal for 24 February that he "went down to printing office after the Court, and corrected *Malachi*. . . . I have certainly bestowed enough of revision and correction." The pamphlet version represents a very substantial rewriting, with a close and steady improvement of phrasing, and the addition of numerous long passages. Some corrections of fact were required; for example the "Falkirk Banking Company" of the *Edinburgh Weekly Journal* became (1. 26) the "Merchant Bank of Stirling". Otherwise, the revisions provide some of the most memorable passages in the pamphlet, and

sentences become transformed by the addition
of some sardonic focussing observation. Such an
example occurs when "Now, this is not fair
construction in our friends, whose intentions in
our behalf, we allow, are excellent, but who
certainly are scarcely entitled to beg the question
at issue without inquiry or discussion" receives
(I. 14) the addendum "or to treat us as the
Spaniards treated the Indians, whom they
massacred for worshipping the image of the Sun,
while they themselves bowed down to that of the
Virgin Mary". There are dozens of similar
additions to the text in the first pamphlet edition,
but limitations of space preclude their being
listed here.

The most noteworthy revision occurs in the
addition of lengthy sections, which have no
equivalent in the *Edinburgh Weekly Journal* text.
The entire story about the *Leetle Anderson*,
based on Scott's acquaintance, Williamson of
Cardona in Peeblesshire, made its appearance
in the first pamphlet edition (I. 29–31), as did
the persuasive section commemorating the former
power of the Scottish peers and Members of
Parliament (II. 45–9).

Not content even with this re-writing, Scott
further corrected the pamphlet in preparation
for its second edition. A copy of the first edition,
with additions in Scott's hand, has survived in
the Blackwood Collection of the National Library

of Scotland.. Scott must have revised this text
during the same days in which he was engaged in
preparing his Second Letter for pamphlet form,
and in drafting his Third Letter for the *Edinburgh
Weekly Journal*. He was now, therefore, able to
think of Malachi's Letters as a whole, and to
make further slight changes in the interests of
accuracy, or of validating his argument, as
when, between the two sentences (1. 27, 1. 3),
we find added in the second edition "The Bank
of Falkirk also became insolvent within these
fifteen years but paid up its engagements without
much loss to the creditors."

Scott's Second Letter, written between 25 and
28 February, appeared in the *Edinburgh Weekly
Journal* for 1 March 1826, pp. 67—70. The first
pamphlet edition was advertised as being published on March 3, with a second edition by 15 March;
and a third had been published by 5 April.

In his Journal for 3 March, Scott laments that
he "could not get the last sheets of *Malachi*,
Second Epistle, last night, so they must go out
to the world uncorrected—a great loss, for the
last touches are always most effectual; and I
expect misprints in the additional matter."
Collation of the available editions shows that there
is no shortage of textual revision; Scott was merely
lamenting his lack of opportunity to reread,
and perhaps further revise, additions which he
had already made to the first stage of proof.

As with the First Letter in pamphlet form, there is a substantial expansion of the text, varying from minor changes of wording to pages of new material. Examples of this wholesale expansion are the comparison with Ireland (11. 57—8), or the amusing and spirited exchange on national differences between Scotsmen and Englishmen (11. 65—71).

Despite these additions, Scott seems to have been far from satisfied with the first pamphlet edition of his Second Letter, and subjected it to a remarkable degree of further revision before the appearance of the second edition. A few of the changes seem to represent an attempt to make the final improvements earlier denied to Scott, as when "Harries, Edderachyles, and Loch Horrible", in 11. 59, becomes "Harries, Edderachyllis, Cape-Wrath, and Loch Erriboll", or "Some Joseph will say", in 11. 84, is corrected to "Some Moses will say". The interests of accuracy required the occasional toning down of an earlier assertion, as when "there was always an Admiral", in 11. 71, reappeared as "there was generally an Admiral".

A number of passages, however, have been augmented in a surprising way by the insertion of several hundred words into the argument. Space prevents a listing here of all the available examples, though it is of interest to note Scott's skill in inserting new material into the existing

structure of his original, as when, between two
sentences (II. 50, l. II), he adds:

> You deprive them of those very notes which
> travel farthest from home, and which return
> most slowly; nay, which, from various causes,
> are subject not to return at all. It is therefore
> in vain to say that thus the profession is left
> uninjured, when it is limited to the issue of
> notes of five pounds and upwards. It might be
> as reasonably stated in a case of mutilation,
> that a man was left in the entire and uninjured
> possession of his hand, the prisoner having only
> cut off his five fingers.
>
> If therefore, the proposed measure shall take
> place, the banker's profession must suffer
> greatly, nay, in its present form, must cease to
> exist.

The textual history of Scott's Third Letter is
much simpler. It was written between 4 and 6
March 1826; the proof was corrected on 7 March,
and it appeared in the *Edinburgh Weekly Journal*
for 8 March, pp. 76–7. The first pamphlet edition
was published on 10 March, and a third edition
was in print by 5 April. Some improvements of
wording were made by Scott for the first pamphlet
edition, and a few longer passages appeared for
the first time, such as (III. 34–5) the paragraph
beginning "I will admit", or (III. 37–8) the
sardonic aside on phrenology. No changes, apart
from a few minor ones in spelling and punctua-
tion, were made in later pamphlet editions of
Scott's Third Letter.

Opposition to the Government's measures

on the currency took several forms. Even while
the bill to discontinue circulation of small notes
was being debated in both Houses of Parliament,
public meetings were being held to voice the
general alarm. Issues of the *Edinburgh Weekly
Journal* for 15 February onwards carry reports of
such meetings in Edinburgh, Peebles, Inveraray,
Kirkcaldy, Beith, and many other places, and of
petitions, signed by Commissioners of Supply,
Justices of the Peace, freeholders, and other
influential persons, presented to Parliament.
Scott attended an Edinburgh meeting on 3 March;
of the six hundred persons present, only one spoke
in favour of the measure. Malachi Malagrowther
alludes to this in his Third Letter (III. 4). In their
original appearance in the *Edinburgh Weekly
Journal* and in their wider circulation in pamphlet
form, Scott's Three Letters became identified
as the most influential statement of Scottish
resentment and hostility to the measure.

Malachi's tracts achieved their object. The
Government backed down ungraciously but
inevitably. By mid-March a select committee was
appointed to "report on the expediency of interfering with the present banking systems" of
Scotland and Ireland. Eventually the Government
promised that the measures should not be applied
in Scotland for six months, then for six years,
and by mid-May surrendered altogether.

The provisions of the Act still applied to

England, and the reorganisation of the banking system brought the institutions of that country closer to those of Scotland. The effect of suppressing the smaller notes was lessened by the existence of coins, and the growth of cheques as a medium of exchange. But this provision was wholly misconceived as far as England was concerned. The English country banks were not the cause of the crisis of 1825–6; most of their business was done with large notes or bills; and there is no evidence that the issue of small notes had had anything to do with their collapse.

Scott's role in this Scottish reverse for the Government was not passed over. Personal attacks on his integrity were made by Lord Archibald Hamilton and Joseph Hume. Lord Melville wrote a bitter reprobation of Malachi's *Letters* to be circulated to his special allies in Scotland. Even Scott's friends were alarmed. Canning opposed his views in the House of Commons, and the Cabinet looked for someone to answer Malachi in the same vein. The then Secretary to the Admiralty, John Wilson Croker, a particular friend of Scott, was persuaded to attack. Two *Letters*, under the pseudonym of E. Bradwardine Waverley, an amalgam of names from Scott's first novel, appeared in the London *Courier*, and were reprinted in pamphlet form, for John Murray (London) and Oliver and Boyd (Edinburgh) in mid-March 1826.

Croker's two *Letters* reply to the first pamphlet edition of Malachi's First Letter, the Second and Third being curtly dismissed in a waspish postscript. Though Croker writes with his usual destructive skill, he provides no plausible answer to Scott's charges. The pamphlets show the immediate seriousness with which the Cabinet took Scott's attack on them, and illustrate the quandary in which Scott's friends found themselves, when the man who "sweetened even the bitter cup of politics with candour and good humour" began to vaunt his "hasty and peevish humour".

In Edinburgh, Scott found gratitude enough. Lauded at public meetings, when the Government abandoned their designs on the Scottish banks, he was credited with the full glory of the victory. As the *Edinburgh Weekly Journal* exclaimed, "If ever an effect was clearly referable to a cause, the Scottish Letters on the Currency accomplished this important result." Scott's service to the Scottish banks is remembered to-day by his prominent appearance on the notes of the British Linen Bank, and its successor the Bank of Scotland.

In December 1830, Scott again assumed the mask of Malachi Malagrowther, to write a Fourth Letter in which he satirically reviled the Reform Bill. Scott's printer and publisher bitterly opposed the pamphlet, and it was never published. But, for the time being, Scott had done with Malachi Malagrowther. The same newspapers which advertised the many pamphlet editions of his Letters also advertised the sale by auction of Scott's Edinburgh house and its furniture. When he was being hailed as the saviour of his nation, Scott was calculating whether the sales of Malachi s Letters might sustain his petty cash, and then turned from the triumphs of national finance to the full revelation of his private ruin.

Stirling   DAVID SIMPSON
March 1971   ALASTAIR WOOD

THOUGHTS

ON THE

PROPOSED CHANGE OF CURRENCY,

AND

OTHER LATE ALTERATIONS,

AS THEY AFFECT, OR ARE INTENDED TO AFFECT,

THE

KINGDOM OF SCOTLAND.

Ergo, Caledonia, nomen inane, Vale!

EDINBURGH:

Printed by James Ballantyne and Company.

FOR WILLIAM BLACKWOOD, EDINBURGH.

1826.

THOUGHTS

PROPOSED CHANGE OF CURRENCY.

OF THE EDINBURGH WEEKLY JOURNAL.

MY DEAR MR JOURNALIST,

I am by pedigree a discontented person, so
that you may throw this letter into the fire, if
you have any apprehensions of incurring the displeasure of your superiors. I am, in fact, the
lineal descendant of Sir Mungo Malagrowther,
who makes a figure in the Fortunes of Nigel,
and have retained a reasonable proportion of his
ill luck, and, in consequence, of his ill temper.
If, therefore, I should chance to appear too warm
and poignant in my observations, you must impute it to the hasty and peevish humour which
I derive from my ancestor. But, at the same

time, it often happens that this disposition leads
me to speak useful, though unpleasant truths,
when more prudent men hold their tongues and
eat their pudding. A lizard is an ugly and dis-
gusting thing enough ; but, methinks, if a lizard
were to run over my face and awaken me, which
is said to be their custom when they observe a
snake approach a sleeping person, I should neither scorn his intimation, nor feel justifiable in
crushing him to death, merely because he is a
filthy little abridgement of a crocodile. Therefore, " for my love, I pray you, wrong me not."

I am old, sir, poor, and peevish, and, therefore,
I may be wrong ; but when I look back on the
last fifteen or twenty years, and more especially
on the last ten, I think I see my native country
of Scotland, if it is yet to be called by a title so
discriminative, falling, so far as its national, or
rather, perhaps, I ought now to say its *provincial,* interests are concerned, daily into more absolute contempt. Our ancestors were a people
of some consideration in the councils of the empire. So late as my own younger days, an English minister would have paused, even in a favour-

ite measure, if a reclamation of national rights had been made by a Member for Scotland, supported, as it uniformly then was, by the voice of her representatives and her people. Such ameliorations in our peculiar system as were thought necessary, in order that North Britain might keep pace with her Sister in the advance of improvement, were suggested by our own countrymen, persons well acquainted with our peculiar system of laws, (as different from those of England as from those of France,) and who knew exactly how to adapt the desired alteration to the principle of our legislative enactments, so that the whole machine might, as mechanics say, work well and easily. For a long time, this wholesome check upon innovation, which requires the assimilation of a proposed improvement with the general constitution of the country to which it has been recommended, and which ensures that important point, by stipulating that the measure shall originate with those to whom the spirit of the constitution is familiar, has been, so far as Scotland is concerned, considerably disused. Those who have stepped forward to repair the gradual failure of our constitutional system of law, have been persons that, howsoever qualified in other respects, have had little farther knowledge of its construction, than could be acquired by a hasty and partial survey, just before they commenced their labours. Scotland and her laws have been too often subjected to the alterations of any person who chose to found himself a reputation, by bringing in a bill to cure some defect which had never been felt in practice, but which was represented as a frightful bugbear to English statesmen, who, wisely and judiciously tenacious of the legal practice and principles received at home, are proportionally startled at the idea of any which cannot be brought to assimilate with them.

The English seem to have made a compromise with the active tendency to innovation, which is one great characteristic of the day. Wise and sagacious themselves, they are nervously jealous of innovations in their own laws —*Nolumus leges Angliæ mutari,* is written on the skirts of their judicial robes, as the most sacred texts of Scripture were inscribed on the phylacteries of the Rabbis. The belief that the Common Law of England constitutes the Perfection of human reason, is a maxim bound upon their foreheads. Law Monks they have been called in other respects, and like Monks they are devoted to their own rule, and admit no question of its infallibility. There can be no doubt that their love of a system, which, if not perfect, has so much in it that is excellent, originates in the most praiseworthy feelings. Call it if you will the prejudice of education, it is still a prejudice honourable in itself, and useful to the public. I only find fault with it, because, like the Friars in the Duenna, these English Monks will not tolerate in their lay-brethren of the North the slightest pretence to a similar feeling.

In England, therefore, no innovation can be proposed affecting the administration of justice, without being subjected to the strict inquiry of the Guardians of the Law, and afterwards resisted pertinaciously until time and the most mature and reiterated discussion shall have proved its

utility, nay, its necessity. The old saying is
still true in all its points—Touch but a cobweb
in Westminster-Hall, and the old spider will
come out in defence of it. This caution may
sometimes postpone the adoption of useful
amendments, but it operates to prevent all hasty
and experimental innovations ; and it is surely
better that existing evils should be endured for
some time longer, than that violent remedies
should be hastily adopted, the unforeseen and
unprovided-for consequences of which are often
so much more extensive than those which had
been foreseen and reckoned upon. An ordinary
mason can calculate upon the exact gap which
will be made by the removal of a corner-stone
in an old building ; but what architect, not intimately acquainted with the whole edifice, can
presume even to guess how much of the structure is, or is not, to follow ?

The English policy in this respect is a
wise one, and we have only to wish they would
not insist upon keeping it all to themselves. But
those who are most devoted to their own religion, have least sympathy for the feelings of dis-

senters ; and a spirit of proselytism has of late
shown itself in England for extending the benefits of their system, in all its strength and weakness, to a country, which has been hitherto
flourishing and contented under its own. They
adopted the conclusion, that all English enactments are right; but the system of municipal law
in Scotland is not English, therefore it is wrong.
Under sanction of this syllogism, our rulers have
indulged and encouraged a spirit of experiment
and innovation at our expense, which they resist
obstinately when it is to be carried through at
their own risk.

For more than one half of last century, this
was a practice not to be thought of. Scotland
was during that period disaffected, in bad humour, armed too, and smarting under various
irritating recollections. This is not the sort of
patient for whom an experimental legislator
chooses to prescribe. There was little chance of
making Saunders take the patent pill by persuasion—main force was a dangerous argument,
and some thought claymores had edges.

This period passed away, a happier one arrived, and Scotland, no longer the object of terror, or at least great uneasiness, to the British Government, was left from the year 1750 under the guardianship of her own institutions, to win her silent way to national wealth and consequence. Contempt probably procured for her the freedom from interference, which had formerly been granted out of fear; for the medical faculty are as slack in attending the garrets of paupers as the caverns of robbers. But neglected as she was, and perhaps *because* she was neglected, Scotland, reckoning her progress during the space from the close of the American war to the present day, has increased her prosperity in a ratio more than five times greater than that of her more fortunate and richer sister. She is now worth the attention of the learned faculty, and God knows she has had plenty of it. She has been bled and purged, spring and fall, and *talked* into courses of physic, for which she had little occasion. She has been of late a sort of experimental farm, upon which every politician has been permitted to try his theory—a kind of common property, where every juvenile statesman has been encouraged to make his inroads, as in Morayland, where, anciently, according to the idea of the old Highlanders, all men had a right to take their prey —a subject in a common dissecting-room, left to the scalpel of the junior students, with the degrading inscription,—*Fiat experimentum in corpore vili.*

I do not mean to dispute, sir, that much alteration was necessary in our laws, and that much benefit has followed many of the great changes which have taken place. I do not mean to deprecate a gradual approach to the English system, especially in commercial law. The Jury Court, for example, was a fair experiment, in my opinion, cautiously introduced as such, and placed under such regulations as might best assimilate its forms with those of the existing Supreme Court. I beg therefore to be considered as not speaking of the alterations themselves, but of the apparent hostility towards our municipal institutions, as repeatedly manifested in the course of late proceedings, tending to force and wrench them into a similarity with those of England.

The opinions of our own lawyers, nay, of our

Judges, than whom wiser and more honourable men never held that high character, have been, if report speaks true, something too much neglected and controlled in the course of these important changes, in which, methinks, they ought to have had a leading and primary voice. They have been almost avowedly regarded not as persons the beşt qualified to judge of proposed innovations, but as prejudiced men, determined to oppose them right or wrong. The last public Commission was framed on the very principle, that if Scotch Lawyers were needs to be employed, a sufficient number of these should consist of gentlemen, who, whatever their talents and respectability might be in other respects, had been too long estranged from the study of Scottish law, to retain any accurate recollection of an abstruse science, or any decided partiality for its technical forms. This was done avowedly for the purpose of evading the natural partiality of the Scottish Judges and practitioners to their own system; that partiality, which the English themselves hold so sacred a feeling in their own Judges, and Counsel learned in the law. I am not, I repeat, complaining of the result of the Commissions, but of the spirit in which the alterations were undertaken. Unquestionably much was done in brushing up and improving the old machinery of Scottish Law Courts, and in making it move more rapidly, though scarce, I think, more correctly than before. Dispatch has been much attended to. But it may be ultimately found, that the time-piece which runs fastest does not intimate the time most accurately. At all events, the changes have been made and established—there let them rest. And had I, Malachi Malagrowther, the sole power to-morrow of doing so, I would not restore the old forms of judicial proceedings ; because I hold the constitution of Courts of Justice too serious matters to be put back or forward at pleasure, like a boy's first watch, merely for experiment's sake.

What I *do* complain of is the general spirit of slight and dislike manifested to our national establishments, by those of the sister country who are so very zealous in defending their own ; and not less do I complain of their jealousy of the opinions of those who cannot but be much better acquainted than they, both with the merits and deficiencies of the system, which hasty and imperfectly informed judges have shown themselves so anxious to revolutionize.

There is no explanation to be given of this but one—namely, the entire conviction and belief of our English brethren, that the true Themis is worshipped in Westminster Hall, and that her adorers cannot be too zealous in her service; while she, whose image an ingenious artist has depicted balancing herself upon a *te-totum* on the southern window of the Parliament House of Edinburgh, is a mere idol,—a Diana of Ephesus,—whom her votaries worship, either because her shrine brings great gain to the craftsmen, or out of an ignorant and dotard superstition, which induces them to prefer the old Scottish *Mumpsimus* to the Modern English *Sumpsimus*. Now, this is not fair construction in our friends, whose intentions in our behalf, we allow, are excellent, but who certainly are scarcely entitled to beg the question at issue without inquiry or discussion, or to treat us as the Spaniards treated the Indians, whom they massacred for worshipping the image of the Sun, while they themselves bowed down to that of the Virgin Mary. Even Queen Elizabeth was contented with the evasive answer of Melville, when hard pressed with the trying question, whether Queen Mary or she were the fairest. We are willing, in the spirit of that answer, to say, that the Themis of Westminster Hall is the best fitted to preside over the administration of the larger, and more fertile country of beef and pudding; while she of the te-totum (placed in that precarious position, we presume, to express her instability, since these new lights were struck out) claims a more limited but equally respectful homage, within her ancient jurisdiction—*sua paupera regna*—the Land of Cakes. If this compromise does not appease the ardour of our brethren for converting us to English forms and fashions, we must use the scriptural question, " Who hath required these things at your hands ?"

The inquiries and result of another Commission are too much to the purpose to be suppressed. The object was to investigate the conduct of the Revenue Boards in Ireland and Scotland. In the former, it is well known, great mismanagement was discovered; for Pat, poor fellow, had been playing the loon to a considerable extent. In Scotland, *not a shadow of abuse prevailed.* You would have thought, Mr Journalist, that the Irish Boards would have been reformed in some shape, and the Scotch establishments honourably acquitted, and suffered to continue on the footing of independence which they had so long enjoyed, and of which they had proved themselves so worthy. Not so, sir. The Revenue Boards, in both countries, underwent exactly the same regulation, were deprived of their independent consequence, and placed under the superintendence of English control; the innocent and the guilty being treated in every respect alike. Now, on the side of Scotland, this was like Trinculo losing his bottle in the pool —there was not only dishonour in the thing, but an infinite loss.

I have heard two reasons suggested for this indiscriminating application of punishment to the innocent and to the culpable.

In the first place, it was honestly confessed that Ireland would never have quietly submitted to the indignity offered to her, unless poor inoffensive Scotland had been included in the regulation. The Green Isle, it seems, was of the mind of a celebrated lady of quality, who, being about to have a decayed tooth drawn, refused to submit to the operation till she had seen the dentist extract a sound and serviceable grinder from the jaws of her waiting-woman—and her humour was to be gratified. The lady was a termagant dame—the wench a tame-spirited simpleton—the dentist an obliging operator—and the teeth of both were drawn accordingly.

This gratification of his humours is gained by Pat's being up with the pike and shilelah on any or no occasion. God forbid Scotland should retrograde towards such a state—much better that the Deil, as in Burns's song, danced away with the whole excisemen in the country. We do not want to hear her prate of her number of millions of men, and her old military exploits. We had better remain in union with England, even at the risk of becoming a subordinate species of Northumberland, as far as national consequence is concerned, than remedy ourselves by even hinting the possibility of a rupture. But there is no harm in wishing Scotland to have just so much ill-nature, according to her own proverb, as may keep her good-nature from being abused; so much national spirit as may determine her to stand by her own rights, conducting her assertion of them with every feeling of respect and amity towards England.

The other reason alleged for this equal distribution of *punishment*, as if it had been the influence of the common sun, or the general rain, to the just and the unjust, was one which is extremely predominant at present with our Ministers—the *necessity of* UNIFORMITY in all such cases; and the consideration what an awkward thing it would be to have a Board of Excise or Customs remaining independent in the one country, solely because they had, without impeachment, discharged their duty; while the same establishment was cashiered in another, for no better reason than that it had been misused.

This reminds us of an incident, said to have befallen at the Castle of Glammis, when these venerable towers were inhabited by a certain old Earl of Strathmore, who was as great an admirer of uniformity as the Chancellor of the Exchequer could have desired. He and his gardener directed all in the garden and pleasure-

grounds upon the ancient principle of exact correspondence between the different parts, so that
each alley had its brother ; a principle which,
renounced by gardeners, is now adopted by
statesmen. It chanced once upon a time that a
fellow was caught committing some petty theft,
and, being taken in the manner, was sentenced
by the Baillie MacWheeble of the jurisdiction
to stand for a certain time in the baronial pillory, called the *jougs*, being a collar and chain,
one of which contrivances was attached to each
side of the portal of the great avenue which led
to the castle. The thief was turned over accordingly to the gardener as ground-officer, to see
the punishment duly inflicted. When the Thane
of Glammis returned from his morning ride, he
was surprised to find both sides of the gate-way
accommodated each with a prisoner, like a pair of
heraldic supporters *chained* and *collared proper*.
He asked the gardener, whom he found watching
the place of punishment, as his duty required,
whether another delinquent had been detected ?
" No, my Lord," said the gardener, in the tone of
a man excellently well satisfied with himself,—
" but I thought the single fellow looked very

awkward standing on one side of the gate-way, so I gave half-a-crown to one of the labourers to stand on the other side *for uniformity's sake.*" This is exactly a case in point, and probably the only one which can be found—with this sole difference, that I do not hear that the Members of the Scottish Revenue Board got any boon for standing in the pillory with those of Ireland—for uniformity's sake.

Lastly, sir, I come to this business of extending the provisions of the Bill prohibiting the issue of notes under L.5 to Scotland, in six months after the period that the regulation shall be adopted in England.

I am not about to enter upon the question which so much agitates speculative writers upon the wealth of nations, or attempt to discuss what proportion of the precious metals ought to be detained within a country; what are the best means of keeping it there ; or to what extent the want of specie can be supplied by paper credit : I will not ask if a poor man can be made a rich one, by compelling him to buy a service of plate, instead of the delf ware which served his turn. These are questions I am not adequate to solve.

But I beg leave to consider the question in a practical point of view, and to refer myself entirely to experience.

I assume, without much hazard of contradiction, that Banks have existed in Scotland for near one hundred and twenty years—that they have flourished, and the country has flourished with them—and that during the last fifty years particularly, provincial Banks, or branches of the principal established and chartered Banks, have gradually extended themselves in almost every Lowland district in Scotland; that the notes, and especially the small notes, which they distribute, entirely supply the demand for a medium of currency; and that the system has so completely expelled gold from the country of Scotland, that you never by any chance espy a guinea there, unless in the purse of an accidental stranger, or in the coffers of these Banks themselves. This is granting the facts of the case as broadly as can be asked.

It is not less unquestionable, that the consequence of this Banking system, as conducted in Scotland, has been attended with the greatest advantage to the country. The facility which it has afforded to the industrious and enterprising agriculturist or manufacturer, as well as to the trustees of the public in executing national works, has converted Scotland, from a poor, miserable, and barren country, into one, where, if Nature has done less, Art and Industry have done more, than in perhaps any country in Europe, England herself not excepted. Through means of the credit which this system has afforded, roads have been made, bridges built, and canals dug, opening up to reciprocal communication the most sequestered districts of the country—manufactures have been established, unequalled in extent or success—wastes have been converted into productive farms—the productions of the earth for human use have been multiplied twentyfold, while the wealth of the rich, and the comforts of the poor, have been extended in the same proportion. And all this in a country where the rigour of the climate, and sterility of the soil, seem united to set improvement at defiance. Let those who remember Scotland forty years since, bear witness if I speak truth or falsehood.

There is no doubt that this change has been

produced by the facilities of procuring credit, which the Scottish Banks held forth, both by discounting bills, and by granting cash-accounts. Every undertaking of consequence, whether by the public or by individuals, has been carried on by such means ; at least exceptions are extremely rare.

There is as little doubt that the Banks could not have furnished these necessary funds of cash, without enjoying the reciprocal advantage of their own notes being circulated in consequence, and by means of the accommodation thus afforded. It is not to be expected that every undertaking which the system enabled speculators or adventurers to commence, should be well-judged, attentively carried on, or successful in issue. Imprudence in some cases, misfortune in others, have had their usual quantity of victims. But in Scotland, as elsewhere, it has happened in many instances that improvements, which turned out ruinous to those who undertook them, have, notwithstanding, themselves ultimately produced the most beneficial advantages to the country, which derived in such instances an addition to its general prosperity,

even from the undertakings which had proved
destructive to the private fortune of the projec-
tors.

Not only did the Banks dispersed throughout
Scotland afford the means of bringing the country to an unexpected and almost marvellous degree of prosperity, but in no considerable instance, save one, have their own over-speculating
undertakings been the means of interrupting that
prosperity. The solitary exception was the undertaking called the Ayr Bank, rashly entered
into by a large body of country gentlemen and
others, unacquainted with commercial affairs, and
who had moreover the misfortune not only to set
out on false principles, but to get false rogues for
their principal agents and managers. The fall
of this Bank brought much calamity on the
country ; but two things are remarkable in its
history : First, that under its too prodigal, yet
beneficial influence, a fine county (that of Ayr)
was converted from a desert into a fertile land.
2dly, That, though at a distant interval, the
Ayr Bank paid all its engagements, and the loss
only fell on the original stockholders. The warning was, however, a terrible one, and has been

so well attended to in Scotland, that very few
attempts seem to have been afterwards made to
establish Banks prematurely—that is, where the
particular district was not in such an advanced
state as to require the support of additional
credit ; for in every such case, it was judiciously foreseen, the forcing a capital on the district
could only lead to wild speculation, instead of
supporting solid and promising undertakings.

The character and condition of the persons
pursuing the profession, ought to be noticed,
however slightly The Bankers of Scotland
have been, generally speaking, *good* men, in the
mercantile phrase, showing, by the wealth of
which they have died possessed, that their credit was sound ; and *good* men also, many of
them eminently so, in the more extensive and
better sense of the word, manifesting, by the
excellence of their character, the fairness of the
means by which their riches were acquired.
There may have been, among so numerous a
body, men of a different character, fishers in
troubled waters, capitalists who sought gain
not by the encouragement of fair trade and honest industry, but by affording temporary fuel

to rashness or avarice. But the number of upright traders in the profession has narrowed the means of mischief, which such Christian Shylocks would otherwise have possessed. There was loss, there was discredit, in having recourse to such characters, when honest wants could be fairly supplied by upright men, and on liberal terms. Such reptiles have been confined in Scotland to batten upon their proper prey of folly and waste, like worms on the corruption in which they are bred.

Since the period of the Ayr Bank, now near half a century, I recollect very few instances of Banking Companies issuing notes, which have become insolvent. One, about thirty years since, was the Merchant Bank of Stirling, which never was in high credit, having been known almost at the time of its commencement by the ominous nick-name of *Black in the West*. Another was within these ten years, the East-Lothian Banking Company. In both cases, the notes were paid up in full. In the latter case, they were taken up by one of the most respectable houses in Edinburgh ; so that all the current engagements were paid without the least

check to the circulation of their notes, or inconvenience to poor or rich, who happened to have
them in possession. Other cases there may have
occurred not coming within my recollection, but
I think none which made any considerable sensation, or could at all affect the general confidence of the country in the stability of the system.

In the present unhappy commercial distress,
I have always heard and understood, that the
Scottish Banks have done all in their power to
alleviate the evils which came thickening on the
country; and far from acting illiberally, that they
have come forward to support the tottering credit of the commercial world with a frankness
which augured the most perfect confidence in
their own resources. We have heard of only
one provincial Bank being even for a moment
in the predicament of suspicion; and of that
copartnery the funds and credit were so well
understood, that their correspondents in Edinburgh, as in the case of the East Lothian Bank
formerly mentioned, at once guaranteed the
payment of their notes, and saved the public
even from momentary agitation, and individuals

from the possibility of distress. I ask what must be the stability of a system of credit, of which such an universal earthquake could not displace or shake even the slightest individual portion?

Thus stands the case in Scotland; and it is clear, any restrictive enactment affecting the Banking system, or their mode of issuing notes, must be adopted in consequence of evils, operating elsewhere perhaps, but certainly unknown in this country.

In England, unfortunately, things have been very different, and the insolvency of many provincial Banking Companies, of the most established reputation for stability, has greatly distressed the country, and alarmed London itself, from the necessary re-action of their misfortunes upon their correspondents in the capital.

I do not think, sir, that the advocate of Scotland is called upon to go farther, in order to plead an exemption from any experiment which England may think proper to try to cure her own malady, than to say such malady does not exist in her jurisdiction. It is surely enough to plead, "We are well, our pulse and complexion prove it—let those who are sick take physic."

But the opinion of the English Ministers is widely different; for, granting our premises, they deny our conclusion.

The peculiar humour of a friend, whom I lost some years ago, is the only one I recollect, which jumps precisely with the reasoning of the Chancellor of the Exchequer. My friend was an old Scottish laird, a bachelor and a humourist— wealthy, convivial, and hospitable, and of course having always plenty of company about him. He had a regular custom of swallowing every night in the world one of Dr Anderson's pills, for which reasons may be readily imagined. But it is not so easy to account for his insisting on every one of his guests taking the same medicine; and whether it was by way of patronizing the medicine, which is in some sense a national receipt, or whether the mischievous old wag amused himself with anticipating the scenes of delicate embarrassment, which the dispensation sometimes produced in the course of the night, I really cannot even guess. What is equally strange, he pressed this request with a sort of eloquence, which succeeded with every guest. No man escaped, though there were few

who did not make resistance. His powers of persuasion would have been invaluable to a minister of state. " What! not one *Leetle Anderson,*
to oblige your friend, your host, your entertain-
er ! He had taken one himself—he would take
another, if you pleased—Surely what was good
for his complaints must of course be beneficial
to yours ?" It was in vain you pleaded your being perfectly well,—your detesting the medicine,
—your being certain it would not agree with you
—none of the apologies were received as valid.
You might be warm, pathetic or sulky, fretful
or patient, grave or serious in testifying your re-
pugnance, but you were equally a doomed man ;
escape was impossible. Your host was in his
turn eloquent,—authoritative,—facetious,—ar-
gumentative,—precatory,—pathetic, above all,
pertinacious. No guest was known to escape the
Leetle Anderson. The last time I experienced
the laird's hospitality, there were present at the
evening meal the following catalogue of guests :
A Bond-street Dandy, of the most brilliant water, drawn thither by the temptation of grouse-
shooting—a writer from the neighbouring bo-
rough, (the laird's *Doer,* I believe,)—two coun-

try lairds, men of reserved and stiff habits—
three sheep-farmers, as stiff-necked and stubborn
as their own halter'd rams—and I, Malachi Malagrowther, not facile or obvious to persuasion.
There was also the Esculapius of the vicinity—
one who gave, but elsewhere was never known
to *take* medicine. All succumbed—each took, after
various degrees of resistance according to his
peculiar fashion, his own *Leetle Anderson*. The
Doer took a brace. On the event I am silent.
None had reason to congratulate himself on his
complaisance. The laird has slept with his ancestors for some years, remembered sometimes
with a smile on account of his humorous eccen-
tricities, always with a sigh when his surviving
friends and neighbours reflect on his kindliness
and genuine beneficence. I have only to add,
that I hope he has not bequeathed to the Chancellor of the Exchequer, otherwise so highly
gifted, his invincible powers of persuading folks
to take medicine, which their constitutions do
not require.

Have I argued my case too high in supposing
that the present intended legislative enactment
is as inapplicable to Scotland, as a pair of elabo-

rate knee-buckles would be to the dress of a kilted Highlander? I think not.

I understand Lord Liverpool and the Chancellor of the Exchequer distinctly to have admitted the fact, that no distress whatever had originated in Scotland from the present issuing of small notes of the Bankers established there, whether provincial in the strict sense, or sent abroad by branches of the larger establishments settled in the metropolis. No proof can be desired better than the admission of the adversary.

Nevertheless, we have been positively informed by the newspapers that Ministers see no reason why any law adopted on this subject should not be imperative over all his Majesty's dominions, including Scotland, *for uniformity's sake*. In my opinion, they might as well make a law that the Scotsman, for uniformity's sake, should not eat oatmeal, because it is found to give Englishmen the heart-burn. If an ordinance prohibiting the oat-cake, can be accompanied with a regulation capable of being enforced, that in future, for uniformity's sake, our moors and uplands shall henceforth bear the purest wheat, I for one have no objection to the regulation. But till Ben-Nevis be level with Norfolkshire, though the natural wants of the two nations may be the same, the extent of these wants, natural or commercial, and the mode of supplying them, must be widely different, let the rule of uniformity be as absolute as it will. The nation which cannot raise wheat, must be allowed to eat oat-bread; the nation which is too poor to retain a circulating medium of the precious metals, must be permitted to supply its place with paper credit; otherwise, they must go without food, and without currency.

If I were called on, Mr Journalist, I think I could give some reasons why the system of Banking which has been found well adapted for Scotland is not proper for England, and why there is no reason for inflicting upon us the intended remedy; in other words, why this political balsam of Fierabras, which is to relieve Don Quixote, may have a great chance to poison Sancho. With this view, I will mention briefly some strong points of distinction affecting the comparative credit of the Banks in England and in Scotland ; and they seem such as to furnish, to one inexperienced in political economics, (upon the transcendental doctrines of which so much stress is now laid,) very satisfactory reasons for the difference which is not denied to exist betwixt the effects of the same general system in different countries.

In Scotland, almost all Banking Companies consist of a considerable number of persons, many of them men of landed property, whose landed estates, with the burthens legally affecting them, may be learned from the records, for the expense of a few shillings ; so that all the world knows, or may know, the general basis on which their credit rests, and the extent of real property, which, independent of their personal means, is responsible for their commercial engagements. In most Banking Establishments this fund of credit is considerable, in others immense ; especially in those where the shares are numerous, and are held in small proportions, many of them by persons of landed estates, whose fortunes, however large, and however small their share of stock, must be all liable to the engagements of the

Bank. In England, as I believe, the number of the partners engaged in a Banking concern cannot exceed five; and though of late years their landed property has been declared subject to be attached by their commercial creditors, yet no one can learn, without incalculable trouble, the real value of that land, or with what mortgages it is burthened. Thus, *cæteris paribus,* the English Banker cannot make his solvency manifest to the public, therefore cannot expect, or receive, the same unlimited trust, which is willingly and securely reposed in those of the same profession in Scotland.

Secondly, the circulation of the Scottish banknotes is free and unlimited ; an advantage arising from their superior degree of credit. They pass without a shadow of objection through the whole limits of Scotland, and are current nearly as far as York, in England. Those of English Banking Companies seldom extend beyond a very limited horizon : in two or three stages from the place where they are issued, many of them are objected to, and give perpetual trouble to any traveller who has happened to take them in change on the road. Even the most creditable provincial notes never approach London in a free current—never circulate like blood to the heart, and from thence to the extremities, but are current within a limited circle ; often, indeed, so very limited, that the notes issued in the morning, to use an old simile, fly out like pigeons from the dovecot, and are sure to return in the evening to the spot which they have left at break of day.

Owing to these causes, and others which I forbear mentioning, the profession of provincial Bankers in England is limited in its regular profits, and uncertain in its returns, to a degree unknown in Scotland ; and is, therefore, more apt to be adopted in the south by men of sanguine hopes and bold adventure, (both frequently disproportioned to the extent of their capital,) who sink in mines, or other hazardous speculations, the funds which their banking credit enables them to command, and deluge the country with notes, which, on some unhappy morning, are found not worth a penny ;—as those to whom the foul fiend has given apparent treasures, are said in due time to discover they are only pieces of slate.

I am aware it may be urged, that the restrictions imposed on those English provincial Banks are necessary to secure the supremacy of the Bank of England; on the same principle on which dogs kept near the purlieus of a royal forest, were anciently lamed by the cutting off of one of the claws, to prevent their interfering with the royal sport. This is a very good regulation for England, for what I know ; but why should the Scottish institutions, which do not, and cannot, interfere with the influence of the Bank of England, be put on a level with those of which such jealousy is, justly or unjustly, entertained ? We receive no benefit from that immense Establishment, which, like a great oak, overshadows England from Tweed to Cornwall—Why should our national plantations be cut down or cramped for the sake of what affords us neither shade nor shelter, and which besides can take no advantage by the injury done to us ? Why should we be subjected to a monopoly, from which we derive no national benefit ?

I have only to add, that Scotland has not felt the slightest inconvenience from the want of specie, nay, that it has never been in request among them. A tradesman will take a guinea more unwillingly than a note of the same value—to the peasant the coin is unknown. No one ever wishes for specie save when upon a journey to England. In occasional runs upon particular houses, the notes of other Banking Companies have always been the value asked for—no holder of these notes ever demanded specie. The credit of one establishment might be doubted for the time—that of the general system was never brought into question. Even Avarice, the most suspicious of passions, has in no instance I ever heard of, desired to compose her hoards by an accumulation of the precious metals. The confidence in the credit of our ordinary medium has not been doubted even in the dreams of the most irritable and jealous of human passions.

All these considerations are so obvious, that a statesman so acute as Mr Robinson must have taken them in at the first glance, and must at the same time have deemed them of no weight, compared with the necessary conformity between the laws of the two kingdoms. I must, therefore, speak to the justice of this point of uniformity.

Sir, my respected ancestor, Sir Mungo, when

he had the distinguished honour to be *whipping*, or rather *whipped boy*, to his Majesty James the Sixth of gracious memory, was always, in virtue of his office, scourged when the King deserved flogging ; and the same equitable rule seems to distinguish the conduct of Government towards Scotland, as one of the three United Kingdoms. If Pat is guilty of peculation, Sister Peg loses her Boards of Revenue—if John Bull's cashiers mismanage his money-matters, those who have conducted Sister Margaret's to their own great honour, and her no less advantage, must be deprived of the power of serving her in future ; at least that power must be greatly restricted and limited.

" Quidquid delirant reges plectuntur Achivi."

That is to say, if our superiors of England and Ireland eat sour grapes, the Scottish teeth must be set on edge as well as their own. An uniformity in benefits may be well—an uniformity in penal measures, towards the innocent and the guilty, in disqualifying regulations, whether necessary or not, seems harsh law, and worse justice.

This levelling system, not equitable in itself, is infinitely unjust, if a story, often told by my poor old grandfather, was true, which I own I am inclined to doubt. The old man, sir, had learned in his youth, or dreamed in his dotage, that Scotland had become an integral part of England,—not in right of conquest, or rendition, or through any right of inheritance,—but in virtue of a solemn Treaty of Union. Nay, so distinct an idea had he of this supposed Treaty, that he used to recite one of its articles to this effect :—" That the laws in use within the kingdom of Scotland, do, after the Union, remain in the same force as before, but alterable by the Parliament of Great Britain, with this difference between the laws concerning public right, policy, and civil government, and those which concern private right, that the former may be made the same through the whole United Kingdom ; but that no alteration be made on laws which concern private right, *excepting for the evident utility of the subjects within Scotland.*" When the old gentleman came to the passage, which you will mark in italics, he always clenched his fist, and exclaimed, " *Nemo me impune*

tacesset !" which, I presume, are words belonging to the black art, since there is no one in the
Modern Athens conjuror enough to understand
their meaning, or at least to comprehend the
spirit of the sentiment which my grandfather
thought they conveyed.

I cannot help thinking, sir, that if there had
been any truth in my grandfather's story, some
Scottish Member would, on the late occasion,
have informed the Chancellor of the Exchequer,
that, in virtue of this Treaty, it was no sufficient reason for innovating upon the private
rights of Scotsmen in a most tender and delicate point, merely that the Right Honourable
Gentleman saw no reason why the same law
should not be current through the whole of his
Majesty's dominions ; and that, on the contrary,
it was incumbent upon him to go a step further,
and to show that the alteration proposed *was*
for the EVIDENT UTILITY *of the subjects within
Scotland,*—a proposition disavowed by the Right
Honourable Gentleman's candid admission, and
by that of the Prime Minister, and contradicted
in every circumstance by the actual state of the

Methinks, sir, our " Chosen Five-and-Forty,"
supposing they had bound themselves to Ministers by such oaths of silence and obedience, as
are taken by Carthusian friars, must have had
free-will and speech to express their sentiments,
had they been possessed of so irrefragable an
argument in such a case of extremity. The sight
of a father's life in danger is said to have restored the power of language to the dumb ; and
truly, the necessary defence of the rights of our
native country is not, or at least ought not to
be, a less animating motive. Lord Lauderdale
almost alone interfered, and procured, to his infinite honour, a delay of six months in the extension of this act,—a sort of reprieve from the
southern *jougs*,—by which we may have some
chance of profiting, if, during the interval, we
can show ourselves true Scotsmen, by some better proof than merely by being " wise behind
the hand."

In the first place, sir, I would have this Old
Treaty searched for, and should it be found to
be still existing, I think it decides the question.
For, how can it be possible, that it should be
for the " evident utility" of Scotland to alter

her laws of private right, to the total subversion of a system under which she is admitted to have flourished for a century, and which has never within North Britain been attended with the inconveniencies charged against it in the sister country ? Even if the old parchment should be voted obsolete, there would be some satisfaction in having it looked out and preserved— not in the Register-Office, or Advocates' Library, where it might awaken painful recollections— but in the Museum of the Antiquaries, where, with the Solemn League and Covenant, the Letter of the Scottish Nobles to the Pope on the independence of their country, and other antiquated documents once held in reverence, it might silently contract dust, yet remain to bear witness that such things had been.

I earnestly hope, however, that an international league of such importance may still be found obligatory on both the *high* and the *low* contracting parties ; on that which has the power, and apparently the will, to break it, as well as on the weaker nation, who cannot, without incurring still worse, and more miserable consequences, oppose aggression, otherwise than by invoking the faith of treaties, and the national honour of Old England.

In the second place, all ranks and bodies of men in North Britain, (for all are concerned, the poor as well as the rich,) should express by petition their sense of the injustice which is offered to the country, and the distress which will probably be the necessary consequence. Without the power of issuing their own notes, the Banks cannot supply the manufacturer with that credit which enables him to pay his workmen, and wait his return ; or accommodate the farmer with that fund which makes it easy for him to discharge his rent, and give wages to his labourers, while in the act of performing expensive operations which are to treble or quadruple the produce of his farm. The trustees on the high-roads and other public works, so ready to stake their personal credit for carrying on public improvements, will no longer possess the power of doing so. The whole existing state of credit is to be altered from top to bottom, and Ministers are silent on any remedy which such a state of things would imperiously require.

These are subjects worth struggling for, and rather of more importance than generally come before County Meetings. The English legislature seems inclined to stultify our Law Authorities in their department ; but let us at least try if they will listen to the united voice of a Nation in matters which so intimately concern its welfare, that almost every man must have formed a judgment on the subject, from something like personal experience. For my part, I cannot doubt the result.

Times are undoubtedly different from those of Queen Anne, when, Dean Swift having in a political pamphlet passed some sarcasms on the Scottish nation, as a poor and fierce people, the Scythians of Britain,—the Scottish Peers, headed by the Duke of Argyle, went in a body to the Ministers, and compelled them to disown the sentiments which had been expressed by their partizan, and offer a reward of L.300 for the author of the libel, well known to be the best advocate and most intimate friend of the existing administration. They demanded also, that the printer and publisher should be prosecuted before the House of Peers ; and Harley, however unwillingly, was obliged to yield to their demand.

In the celebrated case of Porteous, the English legislature saw themselves compelled to desist from vindictive measures, on account of a gross offence committed in the Metropolis of Scotland. In that of the Roman Catholic bill, they yielded to the voice of the Scottish people, or rather of the Scottish mob, and declared the proposed alteration of the Law should not extend to North Britain. The cases were different, in point of merit, though the Scots were successful in both. In the one, a boon of clemency was extorted; in the other, concession was an act of decided weakness. But ought the present administration of Great Britain to show less deference to our temperate and general remonstrance, on a matter concerning ourselves only, than their predecessors did to the passions, and even the ill-founded and unjust prejudices, of our ancestors ?

Times, indeed, have changed since those days, and circumstances also. We are no longer a poor, that is, so *very poor* a country and people ; and as we have increased in wealth, we have become somewhat poorer in spirit, and more loath to incur displeasure by contests upon mere etiquette, or national prejudice. But we have some

merits to plead with England. We have borne
our pecuniary impositions, during a long war,
with a patience the more exemplary, as they
lay heavier on us from our comparative want
of means—our blood has flowed as freely as
that of England or of Ireland—our lives and
fortunes have been as unhesitatingly devoted to
the defence of the empire—our loyalty as warm-
ly and willingly displayed towards the person
of our Sovereign. We have consented with submission, if not with cheerfulness, to reductions
and abolitions of public offices, required for the
good of the state at large, but which must affect materially the condition, and even the respectability, of our over-burthened aristocracy.
We have in every respect conducted ourselves
as good and faithful subjects of the general
Empire.

We do not boast of these things as actual merits ; but they are at least duties discharged, and
in an appeal to men of honour and of judgment,
must entitle us to be heard with patience, and
even deference, on the management of our own
affairs, if we speak unanimously, lay aside party
feeling, and use the voice of one leaf of the holy

Trefoil,—one distinct and component part of the United Kingdoms.

Let no consideration deter us from pleading our own cause temperately but firmly, and we shall certainly receive a favourable audience. Even our acquisition of a little wealth, which might abate our courage on other occasions, should invigorate us to unanimous perseverance at the present crisis, when the very source of our national prosperity is directly, though unwittingly, struck at. Our plaids are, I trust, not yet sunk into Jewish gaberdines, to be wantonly spit upon ; nor are we yet bound to " receive the insult with a patient shrug." But exertion is now demanded on other accounts than those of mere honourable punctilio. Misers themselves will struggle in defence of their property, though tolerant of all aggressions by which that is not threatened. Avarice herself, however mean-spirited, will rouse to defend the wealth she possesses, and preserve the means of gaining more. Scotland is now called upon to rally in defence of the sources of her national improvement, and the means of increasing it ; upon which, as none are so much concerned in the subject, none can be such competent judges as Scotsmen themselves.

I cannot believe so generous a people as the English, so wise an administration as the present, will disregard our humble remonstrances, merely because they are made in the form of peaceful entreaty, and not *secundum perfervidum ingenium Scotorum,* with " durk and pistol at our belt." It would be a dangerous lesson to teach the empire at large, that threats can extort what is not yielded to reasonable and respectful remonstrance.

But this is not all. The principle of " uniformity of laws," if not manfully withstood, may have other blessings in store for us. Suppose, that when finished with blistering Scotland while she is in perfect health, England should find time and courage to withdraw the veil from the deep cancer which is gnawing her own bowels, and make an attempt to stop the fatal progress of her *poor-rates.* Some system or other must be proposed in its place—a grinding one it must be, for it is not an evil to be cured by palliatives. Suppose the English, for uniformity's sake, insist that Scotland, which is at present free from this foul and shameful disorder, should nevertheless be included in the severe *treatment* which the disease demands, how would the landholders of Scotland like to undergo the scalpel and cautery, merely because England requires to be scarified ?

Or again ;—Supposing England should take a fancy to impart to us her sanguinary criminal code, which, too cruel to be carried into effect, gives every wretch that is condemned a chance of one to twelve that he shall not be executed, and so turns the law into a lottery—would this be an agreeable boon to North Britain ?

Once more ;—What if the English ministers should feel disposed to extend to us their equitable system of process respecting civil debt, which divides the advantages so admirably betwixt debtor and creditor—*That* equal dispensation of justice, which provides that an imprisoned debtor, if a rogue, may remain in undisturbed possession of a great landed estate, and enjoy in a jail all the luxuries of Sardanapalus, while the wretch to whom he owes money is starving ; and on the other hand, that a creditor,

if cruel, may retain a debtor in prison for a life-
time, and make, as the established phrase goes,
dice of his bones—Would this admirable recipro-
city of privilege, indulged alternately to knave
and tyrant, please Saunders better than his own
humane action of Cessio, and his equitable process of Adjudication ?

I will not insist farther on such topics, for I
dare say, that these apparent enormities in principle are, in England where they have operation,
modified and corrected in practice by circumstances unknown to me ; so that in passing judgement on them, I may myself fall into the error I
deprecate, of judging of foreign laws without being aware of all the premises. Neither do I mean
that we should struggle with illiberality against
any improvements which can be borrowed from
English principle. I would only desire that
such ameliorations were adopted, not merely
because they are English, but because they are
suited to be assimilated with the laws of Scotland, and lead, in short, *to her evident utility ;*
and this on the principle, that in transplanting
a tree, little attention need be paid to the character of the climate and soil from which it is

brought, although the greatest care must be taken that those of the situation to which it is transplanted are fitted to receive it. It would be no reason for planting mulberry-trees in Scotland, that they luxuriate in the south of England. There is sense in the old proverb, " Ilk land has its ain lauch."

In the present case, it is impossible to believe the extension of these restrictions to Scotland can be for the *evident utility* of the country, which has prospered so long and so uniformly under directly the contrary system.

It is very probable I may be deemed illiberal in all this reasoning ; but if to look for information to practical results, rather than to theoretical principles, and to argue from the effect of the experience of a century, rather than the deductions of a modern hypothesis, be illiberality, I must sit down content with a censure, which will include wiser men than I. The philosophical tailors of Laputa, who wrought by mathematical calculation, had, no doubt, a supreme contempt for those humble fashioners who went to work by measuring the person of their customer ; but Gulliver tells us, that the worst clothes he ever wore, were constructed upon abstract principles; and truly I think we have seen some laws, and may see more, not much better adapted to existing circumstances, than the Captain's philosophical uniform to his actual person.

It is true, that every wise statesman keeps sound and general political principles in his eye, as the pilot looks upon his compass to discover his true course. But this true course cannot always be followed out straight and diametrically; it must be altered from time to time, nay, sometimes apparently abandoned, on account of shoals, breakers, and headlands, not to mention contrary winds. The same obstacles occur to the course of the Statesman. The point at which he aims may be important, the principle on which he steers may be just; yet the obstacles arising from rooted prejudices, from intemperate passions, from ancient practices, from a different character of people, from varieties in climate and soil, may cause a direct movement upon his ultimate object to be attended with distress to individuals, and loss to the community, which no good man would wish to occasion, and with dangers which no wise man would voluntarily choose to encounter.

Although I think the Chancellor of the Exchequer has been rather precipitate in the decided opinion which he is represented to have expressed on this occasion, I am far from entertaining the slightest disrespect for the right honourable Gentleman. " I hear as good exclamation upon him as on any man in Messina, and though I am but a poor man, I am glad to hear it." But a decided attachment to abstract principle, and to a spirit of generalizing, is—like a rash rider on a headstrong horse—very apt to run foul of local obstacles, which might have been avoided by a more deliberate career, where the nature of the ground had been previously considered.

I make allowance for the temptation natural to an ingenious and active mind. There is a natural pride in following out an universal and levelling principle. It seems to augur genius, force of conception, and steadiness of purpose ; qualities which every legislator is desirous of being thought to possess. On the other hand, the study of local advantages and impediments demands labour and inquiry, and is rewarded after all only with the cold and parsimonious praise due to humble industry. It is no less true, however, that measures which go straight and direct to a great general object, without noticing intervening impediments, must often resemble the fierce progress of the thunderbolt or the canon-ball, those dreadful agents, which, in rushing right to their point, care not what ruin they make by the way. The sounder and more moderate policy, accommodating its measures to exterior circumstances, rather resembles the judicious course of a well-conducted highway, which, turning aside frequently from its direct course,

" Winds round the corn-field and the hill of vines,"

and becomes devious, that it may respect property and avoid obstacles ; thus escaping even temporary evils, and serving the public no less in its more circuitous, than it would have done in its direct course.

Can you tell me, sir, if this *uniformity* of civil institutions, which calls for such sacrifices, be at

all descended from, or related to, a doctrine nearly
of the same name, called Conformity in religious
doctrine, very fashionable about 150 years since,
which undertook to unite the jarring creeds of
the United Kingdom to one common standard,
and excited a universal strife by the vain attempt, and a thousand fierce disputes, in which
she

> "———— umpire sate,
> And by decision more embroil'd the fray?"

Should Uniformity have the same pedigree, Malachi Malagrowther proclaims her " a hawk of
a very bad nest."

The universal opinion of a whole kingdom,
founded upon a century's experience, ought not
to be lightly considered as founded in ignorance
and prejudice. I am something of an agriculturist; and in travelling through the country, I
have often had occasion to wonder that the inhabitants of particular districts had not adopted
certain obvious improvements in cultivation.
But, upon inquiry, I have usually found that
appearances had deceived me, and that I had
not reckoned on particular local circumstances,

which either prevented the execution of the system I should have theoretically recommended, or rendered some other more advantageous in the particular circumstances.

I do not therefore resist theoretical innovation in general; I only humbly desire it may not outrun the suggestions arising from the experience of ages. I would have the necessity felt and acknowledged before old institutions are demolished—the *evident utility* of every alteration demonstrated before it is adopted upon mere speculation. I submit our ancient system to the pruning-knife of the legislature, but would not willingly see our reformers employ a weapon, which, like the sword of Jack the Giant-Killer, *cuts before the point.*

It is always to be considered, that in human affairs, the very best imaginable result is seldom to be obtained, and that it is wise to content ourselves with the best which can be got. This principle speaks with a voice of thunder against violent innovation, for the sake of possible improvement, where things are already well. We ought not to desire better-bread than is made of wheat. Our Scottish proverb warns us to *let weel bide;* and all the world has heard of the untranslateable Italian epitaph upon the man, who died of taking physic to make him better, when he was already in health.

I am, Mr Journalist,

Yours,

MALACHI MALAGROWTHER.

POSTSCRIPT.

Since writing these hasty thoughts, I hear it reported that we are to have an extension of our precarious reprieve, and that our six months are to be extended to six years. I would not have Scotland trust to this hollow truce. The measure ought, like all others, to be canvassed on its merits, and frankly admitted or rejected; it has been stirred, and ought to be decided. I request my countrymen not to be soothed into inactivity by that temporizing, and, I will say, unmanly vacillation. Government is pledged to nothing

by taking an open course ; for if the bill, so far
as applicable to Scotland, is at present absolutely laid aside, there can be no objection to their
resuming it at any period, when, from change
of circumstances, it may be advantageous to
Scotland, and when, for what I know, it may
be welcomed as a boon.

But if held over our heads as a minatory
measure, to take place within a certain period,
what can the event be but to cripple and ultimately destroy the present system, on which a
direct attack is found at present inexpedient ?
Can the Bankers continue to conduct their profession on the same secure footing, with an abro-
gation of it in prospect ? Must it not cease to
be what it has hitherto been—a business carried on both for their own profit, and for the accommodation of the country ? Instead of em-
ploying their capital in the usual channels, must
they not in self-defence employ it in forming
others ? Will not the substantial and wealthy
withdraw their funds from that species of commerce ? And may not the place of these be
supplied by men of daring adventure, without

corresponding capital, who will take a chance of wealth or ruin in the chances of the game?

If it is the absolute and irrevocable determination that the bill is to be extended to us, the sooner the great penalty is inflicted the better; for in politics and commerce, as in all the other affairs of life, absolute and certain evil is better than uncertainty and protracted suspense.

EDINBURGH:

PRINTED BY JAMES BALLANTYNE AND CO.

A

SECOND LETTER

TO THE

Editor of the Edinburgh Weekly Journal,

FROM

MALACHI MALAGROWTHER, Esq.

ON THE

PROPOSED CHANGE OF CURRENCY,

AND

OTHER LATE ALTERATIONS,

AS THEY AFFECT, OR ARE INTENDED TO AFFECT,

THE

KINGDOM OF SCOTLAND.

When the pipes begin to play
Tuttie taittie to the drum,
Out claymore, and down wi' gun,
And to the rogues again!

EDINBURGH:

Printed by James Ballantyne and Company.

FOR WILLIAM BLACKWOOD, EDINBURGH.

1826.

LETTER SECOND,

ON THE

PROPOSED CHANGE OF CURRENCY.

———

TO THE EDITOR
OF THE EDINBURGH WEEKLY JOURNAL.

DEAR MR JOURNALIST,

WHEN I last wrote to you, I own it was with the feelings of one who discharges a painful duty, merely because he feels it to be one, and without much hope of his endeavour being useful. Swift says that kingdoms may be subject to poverty and lowness of heart as well as individuals; and that in such moments they become reckless of their own interests, and contract habits of submission, which encourage those who wish to take advantage of them to prefer the most unreasonable pretensions. It was when Esau came from the harvest, faint and at point to die, that Jacob proposed to him his exorbitant bargain of the mess of pottage. There is a deep and typical mystery under the scriptural transaction ; but, taken as a simple fact, the sottish facility of the circumvented heir rather aggravates the unfeeling selfishness of the artful brother, to whom he was made a dupe. The " whoreson Apoplexy" of Scotland may be rather a case of repletion than exhaustion, but it has the same dispiriting effects.

Yet, into whatsoever deep and passive slumber our native country may have been lulled from habits of peaceful acquiescence, the Government have now found a way to awaken her. The knife has gone to the very quick, and the comatose patient is roused to most acute possession of his feelings and his intellect. The heather is on fire far and wide ; and every man, woman, and child in the country are bound by the duty they owe to their native land, to spread the alarm and increase the blaze.

———— Jam proximus ardet
Ucalegon————

The city of Edinburgh has uttered a voice becoming the ancient Queen of the North. The Law Bodies, and the Gentry of Mid-Lothian, have set the example of petitioning Government, and proclaiming their sense of the measure designed; it has been followed in other counties, and I trust to see it soon spread into the smallest burghs, into the most wild districts of Scotland. There are none which the impending misery will not reach—there are no Scotchmen so humble that they have not a share in a national insult, so lowly that they will not suffer from a national wrong—none that are uninterested in maintaining our rights both individually, and as a people—and none, I trust, that have not spirit to do so, by all legal and peaceable means.

I congratulate you, sir, on the awakened spirit of our representatives in the two Houses of Parliament. Our true-hearted Duke of Athole, and Lord Lauderdale, whose acuteness and powers of thinking and reasoning may, without disparagement, be compared with those of any statesman now living, have set an example not to be forgotten; and we know that the slender proportion of aristocracy, which Scotland was left in possession of at the Union, entertain the same patriotic sentiments. We are equally assured of the faith of our representatives in the Lower House, and they on their part may believe they will not serve an ungrateful public. Scotland expects from them the exertions corresponding to their high trust—a trust of which they must render an account to their constituents, and that very shortly. Let every body of electors, from Dumfries to Dingwall, instruct its representative upon their own sentiments, and upon the conduct which they desire he should hold during this great national crisis; and let the Administration be aware, that if any of our Members should desert the public cause on this occasion, they are not like to have the benefit of their implicit homage in the next Parliament. Burns's address to them in jest, is language which may now be held to the Scottish representatives in serious earnest :—

> Does ony great man glunch and gloom,
> Speak out and never fash your thumb ;
> Let posts and pensions sink or soom
>   Wi' those wha grant them ;
> If honestly they cannot come,
>   Far better want them.

I have been told by some cautious friends, that the time for such remonstrances as I do most earnestly recommend to our Scottish representatives, would be now more unfavourable than formerly—so unfavourable, that they represent the case as desperate. Admitting all I had said in my first Epistle, these *douce* men see no resource but in the most submissive acquiescence to the commands of those in whose arbitrary will is now lodged the uncontrolled power to listen to reason, justice, nay, compassion, or to prefer the exercise of their own pleasure to the dictates of them all. Your birthright, say these Job's comforters, will be taken from you at all events by superior numbers. Yield it up, therefore, with a good grace, and thank God if they give you a mess of pottage in return—it will be just so much gain. These desponding persons explain the state of total insignificance into which, they say, we have fallen, by a reference to the Irish Union, which has added an hundred more Members to Parliament; so that the handful assigned to Scotland, (which never possessed a very influential power in the House, so far as numbers go,) must

now altogether lose consideration, in opposition
to the majorities of a peremptory Minister, who,
like the " merciless Macdonald,"

> from the *Western Isle*,
> With Kernes and Gallow-glasses is supplied.

It requires but little arithmetic to compute,
that the fated number, forty-five, bears a less
proportion to six hundred and thirteen than to
five hundred and thirteen, the number of the
House of Commons at the time of the Scottish
Union.   Yet, sir, I am not altogether discouraged with this comfortless prospect.   I think I
can see means of relief arising even out of the
very difficulties of the case.   Let us regard the
matter somewhat more closely.

In the first place, I will consider what we can
do by our present Scottish representation,—our
own proper force.   Next, I will have a friendly
word or two with those same auxiliaries of
Ireland, whom, perhaps, the Sassenagh may
find less implicit followers in the present case,
than my chicken-hearted advisers apprehend.
Lastly, I will address myself to the English
Members, and especially to such who, on great

occasions, prefer the exercise of their own understanding to an absolute and obsequious deference to the dictates of an Administration, however much they may respect the statesmen of
whom it is composed, or are disposed to acquiesce
in the general principles on which they act.

Upon the first point I beg to remind you, that
much greater effect is derived from the decided,
conjoined, and simultaneous exertion of a comparatively small force, than from the efforts of a
more numerous body, not bound together by the
same strong ties of duty and necessity. Battles
have been often gained, and political measures
have been as frequently carried, by the determined urgency, or no less determined resistance,
of a comparatively insignificant number.

Nos numerus sumus, is a logical argument
perfectly understood by an English Minister,
and has had great weight in the scale. I will
give a ludicrous instance of this. There was of
old a certain Nobleman, who, by means of certain boroughs, sent certain members to Westminster, which members, being there, were certain to hold the same opinions with the Noble
Lord, and to vote in the House of Commons

exactly to the same tune as his Lordship in the House of Peers. The Great Man, who was the animating soul of this Holy Alliance, had occasion to ask some favour of Government. It was probably something very unreasonable—at any rate, it was so disagreeable to the Minister, that, I am told, he would as soon have relished the proposal of giving silver for a twenty-shilling note of the Bank of Scotland. The Minister made civil excuses—the Peer observed in reply—*We are seven votes.*—The Minister stopped, cleared his throat, changed his argument.—*We are seven voices*, was again the only answer.—The Great Man, usually flattered, became flatterer in his turn—he conjured—he even threatened.—The Peer was as unassailable, in his numerical proposition, by entreaty or argument, as the sweet little rustic girl in a poem which it is almost sin to parody—

> Whate'er the Minister could say,
> The Noble Lord would have his way,
> And said, *Nay, we are seven.*

They parted on these terms. The Minister retired to rest, and dreamed that he saw the per-

tinacious Peer advancing to storm the cabinet,
after having, like the great magician Kehama,
broke himself up into seven sub-divisions of equal
strength, and by means of this extraordinary
process of multiplication, advancing to his daring
enterprise by seven avenues at once. The vision
was too horrible—and a " private and confidential" note gave the necessary assurance to the
Noble Lord, that the magical number Seven had
as much weight in Saint Stephen's, as Dr Slop
assigns to it in the Catholic mysteries ; so the
seven planets continued to move regularly in
their political orbit.

This is a strong proof, sir, of the *vis unita for-
tior*, and contains a good lesson for our Representatives upon the present occasion. It would
be strange indeed, if they, to whom their country has given her confidence, should hesitate to
save her from dishonour and deep distress, which
may approach nigh to ruin, [I will make my
words good before I have done,] when it is only
necessary that they should be as determined and
inflexible, where the safety of an ancient kingdom is concerned, as the selfish old borough-
jobber and his political friends showed them-

selves pertinacious, in pursuit of some wretched personal object of private advantage.

The Scottish Members of Parliament should therefore lose no time—not an instant—in uniting together in their national character of the Representatives of Scotland. If the scene were to be the British Coffee-House, the hour half past six o'clock P.M., and the preliminaries of business a few glasses of claret to national toasts, I should not have the worse opinion of the sense of the meeting. Their first resolution should be, to lay aside every party distinction which can interfere with the present grand object, of arresting a danger so evident, so general, so imminent. It may be at first an awkward thing for Whig and Tory to draw kindly together; for any of the natural Scottish spirit which is left among us has been sadly expended in feeding a controversy in which we must always play a subordinate part, and these party distinctions have become far too much a matter of habit to us on both sides to be easily laid aside. Indeed, we poor Scotsmen are so conscious that our civil wars are but paltry and obscure episodes in the great political quarrel, that we have usually en-

deavoured to attract attention, and excite an
idea of their importance, by the personal violence
and noisy ferocity with which we wage them.
We, the Whigs and Tories of Scotland, have
played in our domestic quarrels the respectable
part of two bull-dogs, who think it necessary to
go by the ears under the table, because their
blue-sleeved beef-eating masters have turned up
for a set-to. The quadrupeds worry each other
inveterately, while not a soul notices them till
the strife of the bipeds is appeased or decided, and
then the bleeding and foaming curs are kicked separate by their respective owners. We play among
the great *dramatis personæ* the part of *Mob on
both sides*, who enter and scuffle in the back
scene, and shout so that their cries at least may
be heard, since no one will attend to anything
which they say in articulate language. You
may have been a bottle-holder of this kind, Mr
Journalist, to one or other of the great parties.
I am sure I have, and I daresay may have sometimes made mischief, though I have oftener en-
deavoured to prevent it : for, like the good knight
Jacques de Lalain, " *De feu bouter ne voulois-
je etre consentant.* Still, however limited my

share may have been in these jars, I have lived
to see the day when I must regret bitterly my
having had the slightest accession to them,
could I conceive the opinions of so obscure an
individual may have added gall to the bitterness which has estranged Scotsmen from each
other. Let these follies be ended ; and do not
let us, like our ancestors at Falkirk, fall to jea-
lousies among ourselves, when heart, and voice,
and hand, should be united against the foreign
enemy. I was about to eraze the last word ;
but let it remain, with this explanation—that
the purpose of this invasion of our rights is acknowledged to be kind and friendly ; but as the
measure is unauthorized by justice, conducted
without regard to the faith of treaties, and contrary to our national privileges, we cannot but
term the enterprise a hostile one. When Henry
VIII. dispatched a powerful invading army to
compel the Scots to give the hand of their young
Queen Mary to his son Edward, an old Scottish nobleman shrewdly observed, " He might
like the match well enough, but could not brook
the mode of wooing." We equally are sensible

of England's good will, we only do not relish the mode in which it is at present exhibited.

The Scottish Members having thus adopted a healing ordinance, reconciled their party quarrels, or laid them aside for the time, would by that very act decide the fate of their country, and when drinking to concord among Scotsmen of all political opinions,

> In the cup an *Union* shall they throw
> Better than that which four successive kings
> In Britain's crown have worn.

Thus united, sir, their task will be a very easy one. Let each, in his own style, and with the degree of talent, from plain common sense up to powerful eloquence, with which he chances to be gifted, state to administration the sentiments of his constituents, and those of his own breast; let it be perfectly understood that the Representatives of Scotland speak in the name of their country, and are determined, one and all, to see the threatened and obnoxious measure departed from, and till that time to enter into no public business,—I cannot help thinking that such a remonstrance, in a case of vital importance to Scotland, and of such trifling consequence to

England, would be of itself perfectly sufficient. But if not, our Representatives must stand firm. I would advise that, to all such intimations as are usually circulated, bearing, " That your presence is earnestly requested on such an evening of the debate, as such or such a public measure is coming on," the concise answer should be returned, " *We are five-and-forty* ;" and that no Scottish Members do on such occasions attend —unless it be those who feel themselves conscientiously at liberty to vote against Government on the division. Is this expecting too much from our countrymen, on whom we have devolved so absolutely the charge of our rights, the duty of stating our wrongs? We exclaim to them in the language of the eloquent Lord Belhaven —" Should not the memory of our noble predecessors' valour and constancy rouse up our drooping spirits ? Are our brave ancestors' souls got so far into the English cabbage-stock and cauliflower, that we should show the least inclination that way? Are our eyes so blinded— Are our ears so deafened—Are our hearts so hardened—Are our tongues so faltered—Are our hands so fettered, that, in this our day—I say, my countrymen, in this our day, we should not mind the things that concern the well-being, nay, the very being, of our ancient kingdom, before the day be hid from our eyes ?" If there is, among that chosen band, a mean-spirited Scotsman, who prefers the orders of the Minister to the unanimous voice of his Country, imploring the protection of her children, let England keep him to herself. Such a man is deaf even to the voice of self-interest, as well as of patriotism. He cannot be a Scotch proprietor—he hazards his own rents ; he cannot be a Scotchman employed in commerce—he undermines his own trade ; he cannot be a professional person—he sacrifices the law of his country ; he cannot be a Scottish man in spirit—he betrays the honour of Scotland. Let him go out from among us—he is not of us. Let him, I say, remain in England, and we wish her joy of such a denizen. Let him have his title and his pension—for the cur deserves his collar and his bone. But do not let him come back to Scotland, where his presence will be as unwelcome to us, as our reception may be ungratifying to him.

It is needless to say, that what Scotland de-

mands from her representatives in the House of
Commons, she expects, with equal confidence and
ardour, from the small, but honourable portion
of the Upper House, who draw their honours
from her ancient domains. Their ancestors have
led her armies, concluded her treaties, managed
her government, served her with hand and heart,
sword and pen; and by such honourable merit
with their country, have obtained the titles and
distinctions which they have transmitted to the
present race, by whom, we are well assured, they
will be maintained with untarnished honour. A
Scottish Lord will dare all, save what is disho-
nourable; and whom among them could we suspect of deserting the Parent of his Honours, at
the very moment when she is calling upon him
for his filial aid? Sir, I pledge myself, ere I am
done, to give such a picture of the impending
distress of this country, that a Scotsman, and
especially a Scottish nobleman, would need to
take opium and mandragora, should he hope to
slumber, after having been accessary to bringing
it on. If the voice of the public in streets and
highways did not cry shame on his degeneracy,
even inanimate objects would find a voice of re-

probation. The stones of his ancient castle would speak, and the portraits of his ancestors would frown and look black upon him, as he wandered in his empty halls, now deprived of the resort of the rich, and the homage of the vassal. But I have no fear of this. A little indolence—a little indifference—may have spread itself among our young men of rank ; it is the prevailing fashion and fault of the day. But the trumpet of war has always chased away such lethargic humours ; and the cry of their common country, that invocation which Scotland now sends forth from one end of the land to the other, is a summons yet more imperious, and will be, I am confident, as promptly obeyed.

It may be said, that the measures which I venture to recommend to our Scottish representatives, of tacking, as it were, their petition of Rights, to every other measure, and making it, so far as they can, a *sine quo non* to their accommodation with Government, may be the means of interrupting the general business of the empire.

To this objection I reply, *First*, that I only recommend such a line of conduct as an *ultimum remedium,* after every other and milder mode of seeking redress shall have been resorted to, and exhausted without effect. *Secondly,* In case of need it cannot be denied, that the plan proposed is a Parliamentary remedy, and corresponds with the conduct of patriots upon former occasions, when they conceived that the magnitude of the object in view warranted their making the most vigorous efforts to obtain it. *Thirdly,* It will not be difficult to demonstrate, that, whatever prejudice may be suffered from a temporary delay of other business, it will be incalculably less than the evil, which will infallibly ensue upon the obnoxious measure in question being adopted ; an evil, the effect of which cannot be confined to Scotland alone, (for no component part of the empire can have sufferings, which do not extend to the others,) but must reach England and Ireland also. When a limb of the human body is disjointed or broken, the whole frame must feel the effect of it.

But to return to the opinion of my cautious friends, who were of opinion that the proportional numbers of the Scottish Members being so small, compared to those of England and Ireland, no good issue could be hoped from their

exertions, however united, however zealous. I
reply, that their country is entitled to expect
from them resistance in her behalf, not only
while a spark of hope remains, but when that
last spark is extinguished. There is no room for
compromise or surrender. Our statesmen of to-
day must be like our soldiers in ages past—

> They must fight till their hand to the broadsword is glued,
> They must fight against fortune with heart unsubdued.

If they do so, not only will they play the part
of true men and worthy patriots, but they will
procure that sort of weight with their constituents, which will enable them to be useful, and,
with the blessing of God, effectual mediators, in
what, I fear, is likely to prove a very distracted
time and country.

But besides this, I can tell my timorous
friends, as Hotspur does his cautious correspon-
dent,—" Out of this nettle Danger we pluck
the flower Safety." I do not think the Imperial
Parliament, consisting, as it now does, of depu-
ties from every kingdom of the Union, is so
likely to take a hasty and partial view of any
appeal from Scotland, as it might have been

when we had to plead our cause before the Parliament of Great Britain only. I trust we should in no case have been treated unjustly or harshly, and I will presently state my reasons for thinking that we should not ; but, arguing the question on the illiberal and almost calumnious idea, that, if not confuted in argument, we were in danger to be borne down by force of numbers, I should derive hope, not fear, from the introduction of the third Kingdom into the discussion.

Betwixt Scotland and England, Mr Journalist, there have been, as you are aware, ancient causes of quarrel, lulled to sleep during the last fifty years, until of late, when a variety of small aggressions, followed by the present seven-leagued stride, show that perhaps they have not been so fully forgotten by our neighbours, as we thought in our simplicity, and that the English Ministers may not be indisposed to take the opportunity of our torpidity to twitch out our fang-teeth, however necessary for eating our victuals, in case we should be inclined, at some unlucky moment, to make a different use of them. Or, the line of conduct of which we complain, may be compared to a well-known operation resorted

to for taming the ferocity of such male animals
as are intended for domestication, and to be employed in patient drudgery. The animal becomes fat, patient, sleek, and in so far is benefited by the operation ; but had his previous
consent been required, I wonder what the poor
Scotch stot would have said ?

Patrick, my warm-hearted and shrewd friend,
how should you like this receipt for domestication, should it travel your way ? You have
your own griefs, and your own subjects of complaint,—are you willing to lose the power of
expressing them with energy ? You have only
to join with the Ministry on this debate—you
have only to show in what light reverence you
are willing to hold the articles of an Union not
much above a century old, and then you will
have time to reflect at leisure upon the consequences of such an example. In such a case,
when your turn comes, (and come be sure it
will,) you will have signed your own sentence.
You will have given the fatal precedent to England of the annihilation of a solemn treaty of incorporating Union, and afforded the representatives of Scotland vindictive reasons for retaliating
upon you the injury which you aided England

in inflicting upon us. Whereas—step this way, Pat—and see there is nobody listening—why should not you and we have a friendly under-standing, and assist each other, as the weaker parties, against any aggressions, which may be made upon either of us, "for uniformity's sake?" —Your fathers are called by our Scottish Kings, " Their ancient friends of the Erischerie of Eir-land," and for my part I have little doubt that Malachi, who wore the collar of gold, must have been an ancestor of my own. Now, what say you to a league offensive and defensive, against all such measures as tend to the suppression of any just right belonging to either country, in virtue of the Articles of Union respeetively ?— You are a scholar, Pat—

> " *Tua res agitur, proxima cum paries ardet.*"

Between ourselves, Patrick, John Bull is, not unnaturally, desirous of having rather more than his own share in managing the great national coach-and-six. He will drive four-in-hand ; and though he has hitherto allowed you a postilion of your own, yet if you set an example of aiding the gross infringement of the Scottish Union— if you aid England, in her destroying for mere

humour—I beg pardon, for mere " uniformity's sake,"—every little mark of independence which is left us—if you countenance the
obvious desire which exhibits itself to break
down all peculiar privileges due to the separate
nations of the Union, to engross the whole management in Boards, which, sitting in London,
and begirt by Englishmen, are to dispense the
patronage, and direct the improvements, of Ireland and Scotland, you will accelerate your own
then unpitied degradation. What is our case
to-day will be yours the instant you have got a
little tranquillity—are caught napping—and
are in condition to have the aforesaid ceremony
practised upon you without danger—I mean
danger to the operator, for peril to the creature
itself is of no consequence. I see you grasp your
shilela at the very thought ! Enough ; we understand each other : Let us be friends. Patrick aids Saunders to-day ; Saunders pays back
Patrick to-morrow, or I will throw away my
thistle, burn my St Andrew's cross, and disclaim
my country!

But what do I talk of to-day or to-morrow ?
The cause of Ireland is tried ALONG WITH that

of Scotland. She stands, at this very moment, at
the bar beside her Sister, and the prohibitory de-
cree passed against the system of currency, which
has spread universal fertility through Scotland,
is extended to Ireland at the very moment when
she proposed to have recourse to it, as well suited to the improvement of her rich soil, and pre-
mising the extension of means of cultivation,
where cultivation is so greatly wanted, and would
be so productive in the return. I am certain
that I am correct in saying, that, in the course
of last summer, there were several Banking
Companies on the Scottish plan on the point of
being established in different parts of Ireland,
and Scotsmen of experience, capable of understanding and directing such establishments, were
eagerly sought for, and invited over to act as superintendants. Whether the system which had
been so eminently successful in Scotland might be
found quite as well qualified for the meridian of
Ireland, it would be great presumption in me
to decide. But it is very likely that success
would ensue, provided too much were not expected at once, and that the requisite discretion
were used in bounding the issue of notes, and

the grants of credit. More or less probable, it was at least an experiment which Ireland had apparently a perfect right to make, an experiment by which she might reasonably hope to profit ; and if she was willing to undertake it at her own risk, I can conceive nothing more unjust than preventing her from doing so——excepting always the still greater iniquity of interdicting in Scotland a system, the advantage of which has been proved by a century's duration, during all which period it has been attended with advantage, but in the last fifty years with the most brilliant success.

Ireland is therefore called upon to interfere on this occasion, not merely by the chance of standing, at some no very distant period, in the very predicament in which Scotland is now placed, but from the stake which she herself has in the question at issue. She cannot but remember that Rome subjected the free states around her much less by the force which was actually her own, than by the use which she made of those whom she had rendered her tools under the name of auxiliaries. The Batavians were employed in the conquest of Britain, the flower of the Britons were carried off from their native country, that they might help to subjugate the Germans. But such a policy, were it entertained, is not likely to deceive nations in the present age, when statesmen are judged of not more by the measure which they mete to countries less capable of resistance, than by that which they use in dealing towards one upon whom it may not be immediately convenient to inflict the same unjust terms.

Ireland may read her future fate in that of Scotland, as in a mirror. Does she still continue to entertain any wish of imitating the Scottish system? the measure of interdiction about to be passed against her renders it impossible.—Does she still expect to be occasionally consulted in the management of her own affairs? She may lay aside for ever that flattering hope, unless she makes common cause with her sister of Scotland, where every human being in the nation is entreating and imploring that dearest privilege of a free country.—Finally, let us have a word of explanation with England herself.

And first let me say, that although the urgent necessity of the case requires that it should be pleaded in every possible form which its advocates can devise—although I press upon Scotland the necessity of being importunate, steady, and unanimous—although I show to Ireland the deep interest which she also must feel in the question at issue, yet it is to England herself, and to her representatives in Parliament, that, taking upon me, however unworthy, to speak for my Country, when the task is perhaps an obnoxious one, I make my most immediate, and I trust not an ineffectual appeal.

The motto of my epistle may sound a little warlike ; but, in using it, I have only employed the summons which my countrymen have been best accustomed to obey. Saunders, if it please your honours, has been so long unused to stand erect in your honours' presence, that, if I would have him behave like a man, I must (like Sir Lucius O'Trigger backing Bob Acres) slap him on the shoulder, and throw a word in every now and then about his *honour*. But it is not a hostile signal towards you. The drums beat *to arms* and the trumpets sound *Heraus*, as well when the soldiers are called out for a peaceful as for a military purpose. And, which is more to the purpose, the last time the celebrated fiery cross was circulated in the Highlands, (it was in the country of the Grants,) the clansmen were called forth not to fight an enemy, but to stop the progress of a dreadful conflagration which had been kindled in the woods. To my countrymen I speak in the language of many recollections, certain they are not likely to be excited beyond the bounds of temperate and constitutional remonstrance, but desirous, by every effort in my power, to awaken them to a sense of their national danger.

England—were it mine to prescribe the forms, my native country ought to address nearly in the words of her own Mason, mangled, I fear, in my recollection—

> " Sister, to thee no ruder spell
> Will Scotland use, than those that dwell
> In soft Persuasion's notes, and lie
> Twined with the links of *Harmony*."

Let us, therefore, my countrymen, make a proper and liberal allowance for the motives of the Ministers and their friends on this occasion. We ought not to be surprised that English statesmen, and Englishmen in general, are not altogether aware of the extent of the Scottish privileges, or that they do not remember, with the same accuracy as ourselves, that we have a system of laws peculiar to us, secured by treaties. These peculiarities have not, by any question lately agitated, been placed under their view and recollection. As one race grows up, and another dies away, remembrances which are cherished by the weaker party in a national treaty, are naturally forgotten by the stronger, and viewed, perhaps, as men look upon an old boundary stone, half-sunk in earth, half-overgrown with moss, and attracting no necessary attention, until it is appealed to as a proof of property. Such antiquated barriers are not calculated immediately to arrest the progress of statesmen intent upon some favourite object, any more than, when existing on the desolate mountain in their physical shape, such a bound-mark as I have described, always checks the eagerness of a stranger upon the moors, in keen and close pursuit of his game. But explain to the ardent young Southern sportsman that he trespasses upon the manor of another—convince the English statesman that he cannot advance his favourite object without

infringing upon national right,—and, according
to my ideas of English honour and good faith,
the one will withdraw his foot within the boundary of private property, with as much haste as if
he trod on burning marle ; the other will curb
his views of public good, and restrain even those
within the limits which are prescribed by public
faith.   They will not, in either case, forget the
precepts so often reiterated in Scripture, fenced
there with a solemn anathema, and received as
matter of public jurisprudence by the law of
every civilized country—" Remove not the old
land-mark, and enter not into the fields of the
fatherless."   The high and manly sense of justice by which the English nation has been honourably distinguished through the world, will
not, I am certain, debase itself by aggression towards a people, which is not indeed incapable of
defending itself, but which, though fearless of
inequality, and regardless of threats, is yet willing to submit even to wrong, rather than hazard the fatal consequences to be incurred by
obstinate defence, *via facti*, of its just rights.
We make the sense of English justice and
honour our judge ; and surely it would be hard

to place us in a situation where our own sense of general mischief likely to ensue to the empire, may be the only check upon the sentiments which brave men feel when called on to defend their national honour. There would be as little gallantry in such an aggression, as in striking a prisoner on parole.

It is to explain more particularly to the English nation, the real and deep reason which Scotland has to combat the present purpose of Ministers, that I have chiefly undertaken this Second Epistle.

I have stated in my former Letter, that the system respecting the currency, which is now about to be abrogated, has been practised in Scotland for about one hundred and thirty years, with the greatest advantage to the country and inhabitants. I have also shown from the Treaty of Union, that it cannot be altered, unless the preliminary is established to the conviction of Parliament, that the alteration is for the EVIDENT ADVANTAGE *of the subjects in Scotland.* No advantage, evident or remote, has ever been hinted at, so far as Scotland is concerned : it has only been said, that it will be advantageous to

England, to whose measures Scotland must be conformable, as a matter of course, though in the teeth of the article stipulated by our Commissioners, and acceded to by those of England, at the time of the Union. I have therefore gained my cause in any fair Court.

But protesting that I have done enough to entitle me to a judgment, I have no objection to go a step farther; and, taking on myself a burthen of proof, which could not be justly imposed on me, I am willing to explain in a general and popular manner the peculiar nature of the paper currency in Scotland, and especially the guards and protections by which it is secured against such evil consequences as have resulted in England from a system the same in name, but operating very differently in practice.

The people of Scotland are by no means, as a hasty view of their system of currency might infer, liable to be imposed upon, or to suffer loss, through the rash and crude speculations of any man, or association of men, who, without adequate capital and experience, might choose to enter into a Banking concern, and issue their own notes.

The Banking Companies of Scotland, who

take on themselves the issuing of notes, are, no doubt, independent of each other so far as they severally contract with the public; but a certain course of correspondence and mutual understanding is indispensable among themselves, and, in that respect, the whole Banks and Banking Companies in Scotland may be said to form a republic, the watchful superintendence of the whole profession being extended to the strength or weakness of the general system at each particular point ; or, in other words, to the management of each individual Company.

No new Banking institution can venture to issue notes to the public, till they have established a full understanding that these notes will be received as cash by the other Banks. Without this facility, an issue of notes would never take place, since, if issued, they could have no free or general currency. It is not the interest of the established Banks to raise rivals in their own profession, and it is directly contrary to that interest to accept of payment in the notes of a new Company, to whose responsibility there occurs any shadow of doubt. They, therefore, only agree to give currency to such new issues, where satisfactory information has been obtained of the safety of affording it. The public have, in this manner, the best possible guarantee against rash and ill-concocted speculations, from those who are not only best informed on the subject, but, being most interested in examining each new project of the kind, are least likely to be betrayed into a rash confidence, and have the power of preventing a doubtful undertaking at the very outset.

The circulation of a Scottish Banking Company, when once established, cannot maintain itself a week without redeeming its pledge to the Banks which receive its notes, by taking them up, and replacing the value either in the notes of such Banks reciprocally, or in specie. A check is thus imposed, which is continually in operation, and every Bank throughout Scotland is obliged to submit its circulation, twice a-week, in Edinburgh, to the inspection of this Argus-eyed tribunal. Satisfactory information that any distant Banking Companies were leaving the safe and moderate walk of commerce, and embarking their capital in precarious speculations, would very soon draw upon them the suspicion of the moneyed interest at large, and certainly put a period to their existence before it could injure the public.

This important species of check is unknown to the practice of England ; nay, it is probably impossible to establish it there, since the metropolis, which is naturally the common point of union, is nearly inaccessible to the notes of private Banking Companies. In stating a circumstance, not perhaps generally known, I may perhaps remove some of the prejudice which has extended towards the Scottish system, as if exposed to the same inconveniencies with that of the sister kingdom.

The Cash-Credits, as they are called, are a most important feature in our Banking system, and, as I believe, entirely peculiar to it.

The nature of the transaction is the simplest possible. A person, either professional, engaged in commerce or manufactures, or otherwise so situated as to render an occasional command of money convenient, obtains a Cash Account to an extent proportioned to his funds, either by pledging his house, shop, or other real property, or by giving the Bank two sufficient sureties to be answerable for the balance, if any, which shall be due to the Company when the account is closed. The holder of the Cash-Credit is then entitled to draw on the Banker for such sums as he may occasionally need, within its limits. He lodges, on the other hand, with the Bank, such cash as he may from time to time receive from the returns of his business, or otherwise. Interest is calculated on the advances drawn from the Bank at five per cent, on the customer's deposits at three per cent only, and the account is finally balanced twice a-year. The interest varies according to the general rate of the money-market. I have stated it upon the general and legal rate, which it never does or can exceed.

This very simple accommodation is so general through Scotland, that no undertaking of the slightest magnitude is entered into without sufficient funds being provided in this manner, in order that the expense may be maintained without inconvenience until the profits come round. By means of such credits, the merchant carries on his trade, the agriculturist manages his farm, the professional man discharges the advances necessary in his business, and the landed gentleman maintains his credit, and pays his way while waiting for the tardy return of his rents. The trustees who conduct public works have recourse to the same accommodation. Scarce any one who is not too rich to need an occasional ad-

vance, (a case very rare in Scotland,) or too poor
to obtain credit, but is provided and acts upon
some Cash Account of this kind, being a sort of
fluctuating system of borrowing and lending. In
the former case, the customer borrows of the
Bank the advances which he needs, in such sums
and at such times as they are necessary ; whereas, without such mutual accommodation, the
loan must have been borrowed in an entire sum,
and paid up at once, though in the former case
it includes more money than is wanted ; and, in
the latter, the settlement of the whole demand
might be untimely and inconvenient.

Supposing the money lodged to exceed the
amount drawn out, the customer becomes a creditor to the Banker for the balance due to him,
and receives a stated interest for it ; while, at the
same time, it lies as in an ordinary deposit account at his immediate command. This system
is, no doubt, liable, like everything earthly, to
abuse. But the general prosperity of the country, managed almost entirely on such an arrangement betwixt those who deal in capital,
and those who need the use of it, has shown that
the partial abuse bears no proportion to the universal advantage. The system has, in its exer-

cise, been, as Shakspeare says of Mercy, " *twice blessed.*" It has prospered both with the giver and the taker ; and while the holder of the Account has been enabled to derive wealth from schemes which he could not otherwise have executed, the increasing funds of the Banker, and his additional power of serving the country, and aiding, in similar instances, the progress of general improvement, add to the sum of national riches.

It is also to be observed, that the intimate connexion between the Bankers who grant, and the respectable individuals who hold cash-credits, from L.100 to L.1000 and upwards, tends greatly to the security of the former. These customers, of whom each thriving Bank possesses many, are the chief holders and disposers of notes ; and, linked as they are with the Banks who grant the accommodation, by mutual advantage, they have both the interest and credit necessary to quash any unreasonable alarm, and secure the Company against what is called a Run, a circumstance to which Scottish Banks have never been materially exposed, and which is not very consistent with the character of the people.

These undeniable facts afford, so far as Scotland is concerned, a decisive confutation to an

argument which has been advanced, for abroga-
ting the issue of small notes. It has been alleged, that such issues being chiefly in the hands
of the lower classes, these were agitated easily
by rumours, and they became the occasion of the
Runs above-mentioned, by which the Banking
Companies are ruined ; as men are crushed to
death in a crowd, when those around them are
agitated by some cause, very likely a vain one,
of panic terror. In itself, it seems, that depriving men of a lucrative branch of their profession, merely because, under certain circumstances, it may become dangerous to their stability, is very like the receipt of Sheepface in the
farce, who kills his master's sheep to prevent their
dying. But, in Scotland, there exists not the
least approach to the disease, which it seems
necessary to anticipate in so desperate a manner ;
for the apprehended *Runs* on Scotch Banks, by
the holders of small notes, have never taken
place, and, from the assigned reasons, are never
likely to do so. The interference of parties so
much interested, would stop such a headlong
movement, as a strong and well-ordered police
would prevent the fatal agitations of a mob, ere
they trod each other to death.

The general principle of the credits thus granted, is one which, in a poor country at least, or among poor traders, is highly desirable. It affords the farmer, trader, or country gentleman, a convenient and equitable means of pledging their property for a fund of credit to conduct their undertakings. It resembles in principle, though on a much more equitable and liberal footing, the impignoration of moveables, which affords facilities, without which the small, yet indispensable branches of traffic, could not be carried on. Let us, in due humility, follow out a comparison at which our pride might be justly revolted. In London, and other great cities, the market-women, and persons of that description, are constantly in the practice of raising a small credit, by pledging their little articles of value, whether ornaments or wearing apparel, or the like, on which they maintain their trade till Saturday brings the weekly returns, when the ornaments are redeemed from the pawnbrokers, worn perhaps on the Sunday, and returned to *lavender* (as the phrase goes) on the next Monday. It is now many years since some well-disposed and benevolent persons, becoming aware of this practice, were shocked and scandalized at the extent of the interest exacted from these poor people, and made or proposed a law for rendering this course of pawnbroking illegal. Sir, the general mass of misery which was about to attend on the well-meant interference of the legislature, was so evident and so alarming, that the measure was either departed from ere it was completed, or repealed immediately, I forget which.

In the same way, we have in Scotland got into the regular habit of pledging our credit in the manner above described, for the purpose of raising a disposable capital. The advantage obtained by both parties is very equitably balanced; but, were it as iniquitous as that of the most grinding pawnbroker, still habit and manners have rendered it absolutely indispensable to us; and, when a general source of credit is forcibly snatched from a country which has relied on it so long, you literally wrest the crutch from the infirm, because, in your mind, it is not of a handsome fashion.

After all, is it not just that we, the party concerned, should be admitted to have a preponderating vote in this matter? If we eventually suffer by adhering to an old and tried system, we can blame no one, but must suffer for our own obstinacy; but if Scotland is to be reduced to distress by having a system forced upon her which she is unable to maintain or carry on, who is to answer for the evils it may bring upon us?

It is by the profit arising upon issuing their small notes, that the Bankers are enabled to make the beneficial advances which custom has now rendered nearly indispensable to the carrying on business of almost any kind in Scotland. Above all, without that profit, the Bankers could not, as hitherto, continue to allow a rateable interest on money deposited in their hands. Let us take a hasty view of some of the advantages attached to this peculiarity of the system.

The general convenience of the Banker affording interest upon deposits is obvious. It is much more convenient to the individual to receive some interest for his ready cash, than that it should lie idle in his desk; and its being thus put into a productive state, instead of remaining an unproductive capital, must be much more useful to the country. This needs no commentary.

It has, besides, tended much to the diminution of crime in Scotland. We have forgot the period preceding the Banking system, but it is easily recalled. Look at the old magazines or newspapers, during the time when the currency was chiefly maintained by specie, a ready temptation to the ruffian—the murder of graziers and dealers returning from fairs where they had sold their cattle, was a not unfrequent occurrence. Farm-houses of the better class, as well as gentlemen's baronial residences, were defended by bars on the windows, upper and under, like those of a prison ; yet these houses were often broken open by daring gangs, to possess themselves of the hoards which the tenant must have then kept beside him against rent-day, and his landlord, for the current expense of his household. At present—*Cantabit vacuus*—the drover or grazier has a Banker's receipt for the price of his cattle in the old almanack, which serves him for a pocket-book, and fears no robbery—while the farm-house, or manor, is secure from the attack of ruffians, who are like to find no metal more precious than the tongs and poker.

Passing over the tendency of the present system to prevent crime, I come to its influence in recommending industry and virtue ; and I am

confident in stating, that the degree of morali-
ty, sobriety, and frugality, which is admitted
to exist in Scotland, has been much fostered,
though certainly not entirely produced, by the
Banks' allowing interest on small sums, which,
if the present prohibitory measure passes, they
will be no longer in a capacity to afford.   Let
the effect of such a violent change be considered
merely in respect to the lowest order of deposi-
tors, who lodge in the Bank from the sum of
ten pounds to fifty.   The first motive to save
among petty tradesmen, mechanics, farm-ser-
vants, domestics, and the like, is the delight of
forming a productive capital ; and in that class,
the habit of saving and of frugality is the foundation of a sober, well-regulated, and useful society. Every judicious farmer scruples to repose
perfect reliance in a farm-servant or a labourer,
till he knows that he is possessed of a capital of
a few pounds in some neighbouring Bank ; and
when that is once attained, the man becomes
tenfold steady and trustworthy. Instances have
occurred, to my certain knowledge, before the
time of the Saving-Banks, where the master,
to hasten this advantageous step in his depen-

dent's life, would advance a servant of character
a little money to complete a deposit, when the
man's savings did not amount to ten pounds,
which is the least sum received by the Banks.
And, by the way, it is not easy to see how these
excellent institutions, the Saving-Banks themselves, can be continued in Scotland, if interest
is no longer allowed by the general Bank ; for
we are at too great a distance to avail ourselves
of the Public Funds for that purpose.

At any rate, the cessation of payment of interest by the Banks, attendant on the abolish-
ing the issue of small notes, would greatly injure, if not effectually destroy, the formation of
those virtuous and frugal habits, which are as
essential to the class of society a little richer
than that to which the Saving-Banks apply, as
to the inferior description to whom these invaluable institutions afford encouragement and
protection.

What is a poor hind or shepherd to do with his
L.20 or L.30, the laborious earnings of his life,
and which he looks to, under God, for keeping
his widow and family from the parish, if Bankers
can no longer afford him some interest for the

use of it ? Where is he to get decent security for his petty capital ? He will either be swindled out of it by some rascally attorney, or coaxed to part with it to some needy relation—in either case, never to see it more. It is difficult enough, even at present, for masters, who take an interest in their servants' welfare, to get them to place their money safe in the Bank ; if this resource is taken away, where is it to be lodged, with any chance of security ? But I think I can guess its fate, friend Journalist. The Banks will be returning on the hands of the shepherd or farm-servant his deposit, just at the time when they are unwillingly distressing his master for the balance on his Cash Account, called up before his well-judged, but half-executed improvements, undertaken on the faith of the continued credit, have become productive. The farmer will, in the hour of need and pressure, borrow the petty capital of his servant ; he will be unable to repay it ; and then, when the distress becomes chin-deep, they may turn beggars together—for uniformity's sake.

If that settling day should ever come, Mr Journalist, when the Bankers, dunned for deposits in their hands, are compelled to be as rigorous with those who have received advances from them—that awful day, when the hundreds of thousands, nay millions, hitherto divided between the Banks and the Public, must be all called up at once, and accounts between them closed—that settling day will be remembered as long in Scotland as ever was the Mirk Monday !

But what can the Bankers do ? Their whole profession must undergo a universal change, that discounts and every species of accommodation may be brought within the narrowest possible limits. At present, the profits divided among the profession, upon perhaps a Million and a Half of small notes, enable them to advance liberally to individuals upon any reasonable security. But if the Banker's occupation is henceforth to consist in stocking himself with a great abundance of gold, and for that purpose engaging in an eternal struggle, not to *preserve* (for that is impossible), but to *restore* an eternally vacillating proportion betwixt the metallic circulation and the wants of the country, such expensive labour ALONE will be likely to prove quite enough for his talents and funds.

The injury done to the Bankers, by depriving

them of such a principal and profitable branch
of their profession, is not to be passed over in
silence. The English are wont, in other cases,
to pay particular heed ere they alter any peculiar
state of things, upon the faith of which property
has been vested in a fixed and permanent line of
employment. But this proposed enactment will
go as far as the in-calling of One Million and a
Half of notes can do, to destroy the emoluments
of the profession. We cannot, as a nation, afford
to be deprived of such an honourable and profitable means of settling our sons in the world.
We cannot afford to lose a resource, which has
proved to so many respectable and honourable
families a means *ad reædificandum antiquam
domum*, and which has held out to others a
successful mode of elevating themselves, by liberal and useful industry, to the possession of
wealth, at once to their own advantage and to
that of Scotland. Thus it must needs be, if the
proposed measure should pass; and when we
come to count the gains we shall then have made,
by change from a paper circulation to one in
specie, I doubt it will form a notable example of
the truth of the proverb, " That gold may be
bought too dear."

The Branches established by Banks in remote parts of Scotland must be given up. The parent Banks would vainly exhaust themselves in endeavouring to draw specie from London, and to force it, at any expense, into more fertile districts of Scotland, which, of course, would receive it in small quantity, and pay for it at a heavy charge. But as to the remote and sterile regions, it must be with the Highlands and Isles of Scotland, as it is now in some remote districts of Ireland, where scarce any specie exists for the purpose of ordinary currency, and where, for want of that representative for value, or paper money in its stead, men are driven back to the primitive mode of bartering for everything —the peasant pays his rent in labour, and the fisher gets his wages in furnishings. Misery is universal—credit is banished—and with all the bounties of nature around them, ready to reward industry—the sinews of that industry are hewn asunder, and man starves where Nature has given abundance!

Great Britain would be then somewhat like the image in Belteshazzar's dream. London, its head, might be of fine gold—the fertile provinces of England, like its breast and arms, might be of silver—the southern half of Scotland might acquire some brass or copper—but the northern provinces would be without worth or value, like the legs, which were formed of iron and clay. What force is to compel gold to circulate to these barren extremities of the island, I cannot understand; and, when once forced there, I fear its natural tendency to return to the source from which it is issued will render all efforts to detain it as difficult as the task of the men of Gotham, when they tried to hedge in the cuckoo. Our Bankers, or such as may continue in the profession under the same name, but with very different occupation and prospects, will be condemned to the labour of Sisyphus,—eternally employed in rolling a cask of gold up a Highland hill, at the risk of being crushed by it as the influence of gravity prevails, and it comes rolling down upon their heads.

Mrs Primrose, wife to the excellent Vicar of Wakefield, carried on a system of specie, with respect to her family, at a much cheaper rate than that at which Scotland will be able, I fear, to accomplish the same object. " I gave each of them a shilling," says the good man, speaking of his daughters, " though for the honour of the family it must be observed, that they never went without money themselves; as my wife always generously let them have a guinea each to keep their pockets, but with strict injunctions *never to change it*." Our state is not so favourable, Mr Journalist. We shall be obliged to lay out our guinea every morning of our lives, and to buy back another every evening, at an increasing per centage, to pay the expense of the next day. Moreover, Mrs Primrose was more reasonable (begging pardon for the expression) than our English friends; for, although she enforced the specie system in her own family, we do not hear that she was ever desirous to intrude it into that of Neighbour Flamborough.

I do not mean to enter into the general question of the difference betwixt the circulation of specie and of paper money. I speak of them relatively, as applicable to the wants and wishes' of Scotland only. Yet, I must say, it seems strange, that, under a liberal system, of which freedom of trade is the very soul, we should be loaded with severe restrictions upon our own national choice, instead of being left at liberty to adopt that representative of value, whether in gold or paper, that best suits our own convenience!

To return to the remote Highlands and Islands, Mr Journalist, I need not tell you that they are inhabited by a race of men, to use Dr Currie's phrase, " patient of labour and prodigal of life," for succouring whose individual wants the tenth part of an English coal-heaver's wages would be more than enough, but yet who are human creatures, and cannot live without food—who are men, and entitled to human compassion—Christians, and entitled to Christian sympathy. But their claims as men and Christians are not all they have to proffer to administration and to England. The distress to which they are about to be exposed will return upon the state at large in a way very little contemplated.

Those sterile and remote regions have been endowed by Providence with treasures of their own, gained from the stormy deep by their hardy inhabitants. The fisheries in the distant Highlands and Isles, under the management of an enlightened Board, have at length accomplished what was long the warmest wish of British patriots, and have driven the Dutch out of all ri-

valry in this great branch of national industry.
The northern fisheries furnish exports to our colonies and to the Continent, exceeding half a
million of money annually, and give employment to a very great number of hardy seamen.
The value of such a plentiful source of prosperity, whether considered as supplying our navy
or affecting our manufactures, is sufficiently obvious. Now observe, Mr Journalist, how these
fisheries are at present conducted.

The branches of those obnoxious establishments, the Scottish Banks, maintained at convenient and centrical points in the north of
Scotland, furnish all the remote and numerous
stations where the fisheries are carried on, with
small notes and silver for payment of the actual
fishers' labour, and in return accept the bills
of the fish-curers upon the consignees. This
they do on the principle of a moderate profit ;
on which principle alone private industry, and
enterprise, and capital, can be made conducive
to the public good. The small notes thus circulated in the most distant parts of Scotland,
return indeed in process of time to the Banks
which issued them ; but the course of their re-

turn is so slow and circuitous, that the interest accruing on them during their absence amply reimburses the capitalist for the trouble and risk which attend the supply. But let any man who knows the country, or will otherwise endeavour to conceive its poverty and sterility, imagine if he can, the difficulties, expense, and hazard, at which gold must be carried to points where it would never have voluntarily circulated, and from whence, unless detained in some miser's hoard, (a practice which the currency in specie, and disuse of interest on deposits, is likely to revive,) it will return to London with the celerity of a carrier-pigeon.

The manufacture of Kelp, which is carried on to an immense extent through all the shores and Isles of the Highlands, supporting thousands of men with their families, who must otherwise emigrate or starve, and forming the principal revenue of many Highland proprietors, is nearly, if not exactly, on the same footing with the fisheries; is carried on chiefly by the same medium of circulation; and, like them, supplied by the Bankers with a circulating medium of small notes, at a reasonable profit to themselves, and with the utmost advantage to the country and its productive resources.

Referring once more to the state of misery in the distant districts of Ireland, I must once more ask, if these things be done in the green tree, what shall be done in the dry tree? If the want of circulation creates poverty and misery in the comparatively fertile country of Ireland, what is to become of those barren deserts, where even at present the hardest labour which the human frame can endure is necessary to procure the most moderate pittance on which human life can be supported? The inhabitants are now healthy, enterprising, laborious; and their industry, producing means of existence to themselves, is of immense profit to their country. If their means of obtaining the payment of their labour is destroyed, nay even interrupted, the state must either feed idle paupers, who once flourished a hardy and independent race of labourers, or it must be at the expense of transporting the inhabitants to Canada and New South Wales, and leave totally waste a country, which few but those bound to it by the *Amor patriæ* will desire to reside in, even if the means of procuring subsistence were left unimpaired.

Can anything short of the UTMOST NECESSITY justify an experiment which threatens to depopulate a part of the empire, and destroy the happiness of thousands ? and how can such a necessity exist, without the least symptom of its having been felt or suspected during the last hundred and thirty years, when the present system has been in exercise ?

Destroy the existing conduit, and let me again inquire, what forcing-pump, what new-invented patent pressure, were it devised by Bramah himself, is to compel specie into these inaccessible regions ?   The difficulty of conveying the supplies is augmented by the risk of carrying wealth unguarded through the regions of poverty.   I know my countrymen are indifferent honest, as Hamlet says ; yet I would not advise the Genius of the specie system to travel through Scotland, moral as the country is, after the fashion of the fair pilgrim, " rich and rare," in Moore's beautiful melody, just by way of trying the honesty of the inhabitants.   Take my

word for it, the absence of temptation is no valueless guardian of virtue. If convoys of gold must
be sent through lonely mountains, I venture to
say, that smugglers will be converted into robbers, and that our romance-writers need not
turn back to ancient times for characters like
John Gunn, or Rob Roy Macgregor.

This I am sure of, that if the mere authority
of a legislative enactment can force a sufficient
quantity of gold into those parts, to carry on the
fishery and kelp manufactures, it can do a great
deal more in favour of the poor but hardy inhabitants. Why should our statesmen be so stint-
ed in their bounty, if it depends merely on legislative enactment ? Why not enact, that whereas the dress now worn by his Majesty's loving
inhabitants of the Lewis, Uist, Harries, Edderachyles, and Loch Horrible, is scanty, thin, and in-
decorous, each inhabitant of these districts should
in future wear a full-trimmed suit of black silk,
or velvet ; and, as his only representative of
wealth has been hitherto a crumpled dog's-ear'd
piece of Scotch paper, that, in future, he never
presume to stir out of his cabin without having,
and bearing about his person, the sum of at least

five golden sovereigns ? The working the stuffs may be a means of relieving the starving weavers of Spitalfields, and the clothes could be conveniently enough forwarded by the escorts who are to protect the chests of specie.

It is not amiss to observe that this violent experiment on our circulation—demanded by no party in Scotland—nay, forced upon us against the consent of all who can render a reason, fraught with such deep ruin if it miscarry, and holding forth no prospect whatever of good even should it prove successful,—can only be carried on at a very considerable expense to England. She must coin for the service of Scotland at least a million and a half of specie—sustain the loss of tear and wear—the chance of accident and plunder—of disappearance by pilfering and hoarding—and be at the expense of supplying this immense quantity of precious metals, not for the benefit, but for the probable ruin, of our devoted country. It is fairly forcing gold down our throats, as little to our advantage, as when the precious metal was sent in a molten state down the gullet of Cyrus, or Crassus,—I forget which.

No argument has been alleged by the English statesmen for pressing this measure, but that of " uniformity ;" by virtue of which principle, a little more extended, they may introduce the Irish Insurrection Law into England to-morrow, and alter the whole national law of Scotland the day after. This argument, I therefore think, proves a little too much, and is, in consequence, no argument at all. In absence of avowed motives, and great darkness as to any imaginable cause, men's minds have entertained very strange and wild fancies, to account for the zeal with which this obnoxious measure is driven forward. Some, who would be thought to see farther into a mill-stone than others, pretend the real reason is to soothe the jealousy of the Bank of England, by preventing the possibility of Scots notes passing in England.—Can it be conceived that our dearest interests are to be tampered with for such an object as this ?—It is very true, that in the adjacent counties of England, innkeepers for courtesy, and drovers and others dealing at Scots fairs, on account of convenience, readily accept of Scots notes in payment ; but that notes, which nobody is obliged to accept, and which the English Banks re-

fuse to change, can circulate to such an extent
as to alarm the Bank of England !—why, sir,
I will as soon believe, that, during the old wars,
the city of London beat to arms, called out their
Trained-bands, and manned their walls, because
the Teviotdale Borderers had snapped up a herd
of cattle in Northumberland. What becomes
of the comparative excellence of the specie circulation to be established in England, if apprehensions are entertained that it cannot stand its
ground against the reprobated paper system of
Scotland ? In God's name, are they afraid people
will prefer paper to gold—leaving, like Hamlet's
misjudging mother, the literally golden meads
of England, to batten on a Scottish moor ? It
is like the ridiculous story told, that there is a
bye-law, or at least a private understanding,
that no Scotsman shall be chosen a Director of
the Bank of England, lest you should find our
countrymen engross the whole management in
the course of a few years.—Why, sir, these opinions remind one of the importance attached to
the fated Stone in Westminster Abbey, of which
it is said, that the Scots shall reign wheresoever
it is carried. But, sir, we must not swallow
such flattering compliments. The Bank of Eng-

land jealous of the partial circulation of a few Scottish notes in the north of England ! ! ! Sir, it would be supposing the blessed sun himself jealous of a gas-light manufactory.

A few general observations on England's late conduct to us, and I will release you.

A very considerable difference may be remarked within these twenty-five years in the conduct of the English towards such of the Scotch individuals, as either visit the metropolis as mere birds of passage, or settle there as residents. Times are much changed since the days of Wilkes and Liberty, when the bare suspicion of having come from North of the Tweed, was a cause of hatred, contempt, and obloquy. The good nature and liberality of the English seem now even to have occasioned a re-action in their sentiments towards their neighbours, as if to atone for the national prejudices of their fathers. It becomes every Scotsman to acknowledge explicitly and with gratitude, that whatever tenable claim of merit has been made by his countrymen for more than twenty years back, whether in politics, arts, arms, professional distinction, or the paths of literature; it has been admitted by the English, not only freely, but with partial favour. The requital of North Britain can be little more than good wishes and sincere kindness towards her southern Sister, and a hospitable welcome to such of her children as are led by curiosity to visit Scotland. To this ought to be added the most grateful acknowledgment.

But though this amicable footing exists between the public of each nation, and such individuals of the other as may come into communication with them, and may God long continue it—yet, I must own, the conduct of England towards us as a kingdom, whose crown was first united to theirs by our giving *them* a King, and whose dearest national rights were surrendered to them by an incorporating Union, has not been of late such as we were entitled to expect.

There has arisen gradually, on the part of England, a desire of engrossing the exclusive management of Scottish affairs, evinced by a number of circumstances, trifling in themselves, but forming a curious chain of proof when assembled together ; many of which intimate a purpose to abate us, like old Lear, of our train, and to accustom us to submit to petty slights and mortifications, too petty perhaps individually to afford subject of serious complaint, but which, while they tend to lower us in our own eyes, seem to lay the foundation for fresh usurpations, of which this meditated measure may be an example.

This difference of treatment, and of estimation, exhibited towards *individuals* of the Scottish nation, and to the *nation itself* as an aggregate, seems at first sight an inconsistency. Does a Scotchman approach London with some pretension to character as a Preacher, a Philosopher, a Poet, an Economist, or an Orator, he finds a welcome and all-hail, which sometimes surprises those whom he has left on the northern side of the Tweed,—little aware, perhaps, of the paragon who had emigrated, till they heard the acclamations attending his reception—Does a gentleman of private fortune take the same route, he finds a ready and voluntary admission into the class of society for which he is fitted by rank and condition—Is the visitor one of the numerous class who wander for the chance of improving his fortunes, his character as a Scotsman is supposed to contain the desirable qualities of information, prudence, steadiness, moral and religious feeling, and he obtains even a preference among the Southern employers, who want confidential clerks, land-stewards, head-gardeners, or fit persons to occupy any similar situation, in which the quality of trust-worthiness is demanded.

But, on the other hand, if the English states-man has a point of great or lesser consequence to settle with Scotland *as a country*, we find him and his friends at once seized with a jea-lous, tenacious, wrangling, overbearing humour, and that they not only insist upon conducting the whole matter according to their own will, but are by no means so accessible to the pleas of reason, justice, and humanity, as might be expected from persons in other cases so wise and liberal. We cease at once to be the North-ern Athenians, according to the slang of the day—the moral and virtuous people, who are practically and individually esteemed worthy of especial confidence. We have become the cater-pillars of the island, instead of its pillars. We seem to be, in their opinion, once more transmuted into the Scots decribed by Churchill—a sharp sharking race, whose wisdom is cunning, and whose public spirit consists only in an illiberal nationality, inclining us, by every possible exertion of craft, to obtain advantage at the expense of England.

Sir, the Englishman, in his natural movements, is liable to an internal sense of suspicion, that the qualities of frankness and generosity are rare. He will always *give* willingly, but he often becomes shabby and litigious in making a bargain. John Bull is in these points exactly similar to his own Hotspur, who, in his dispute with Glendower about the turning of the Trent, exclaims,—

" I do not care—I'll give thrice so much land
To any well-deserving friend ;
But in the way of *bargain,* mark ye me,
I'll cavil on the ninth part of a hair."

The Continent has seen John in both these moods ; and not being able to understand the cause of the change, has been apt to suppose his habits are entirely altered; whereas they see only the same man in two different and extreme humours; in one of which he would willingly relieve a begging vagabond, because the rascal must live; and in the other, will hardly be brought to pay the bill of a poor tradesman, because he is afraid of being over-reached. The ancient and modern mode in which the English travellers did, and do now, pay their ordinary bills on the Continent, are an example of this piebald humour:—Formerly John travelled *en prince*, and even overlooked any species of imposition in innkeepers and *valets-de-place*, as not worth the care of *un homme tel que lui*. Now, he insists upon a preliminary contract, and, neither for love of money, nor for want of money, but from a feverish apprehension that he may possibly be cheated in a reckoning, goes so miserably to work, that all the world cries " Shame on him !" *

To the better, more natural, more predomina-

---

* See the amusing work, called " The English in Italy."

ting disposition of our neighbours, I am well disposed to ascribe the many marks of partiality
and kindness shown to individual Scotsmen by
the English at large—to the latter suspicious,
dogged, illiberal determination to have the best
of the bargain,—that ungracious humour, which
forgets even justice as well as liberal feelings, for
fear their goodnature should be imposed upon,—
I am compelled to ascribe much of their recent
behaviour in international discussions. In such
fits of jealousy, men are like those who wear
green spectacles. Every object they look upon
is tinged with the predominant colour, which
exists not in the objects themselves, but in the
medium through which they are viewed. Talk
to an English statesman of the fairest, the most
equitable proposal for the advancement of Scotland as a nation, the most just and indisputable
claim on behalf of her public establishments or
functionaries, the idea of a *Scotch Job* starts up
like an apparition, and frightens all power of
equitable decision out of the Minister's head.
It is in vain urged, that even the expense of the
proposed measure must be discharged by Scotland herself—her Sister is ready with the school-

boy's answer to his Fag,—" All that is *yours* is *ours*, and all *ours* is *our own*." Let the scales of Justice be trimmed with the nicest exactness if you will, but do not let Authority throw the sword into the scale from mere apprehension, lest, after having done her utmost to secure the advantage, she be cheated in the weighing.

In an old Scottish law, to be convicted of being an Egyptian, or gipsy, was equivalent to conviction that the party was a common and notorious thief. And truly the English seem to think, (in public matters, though by no means in private relations,) that being a Scotsman is equivalent to being an embezzler of public money, a jobber, and a peculator. But when they suppose that we are able and willing in all such cases to impose on them, they do injustice alike to their own shrewdness and our integrity.

It arises out of this unhappy state of feeling towards us, more than to any actual desire of giving us offence, that England has of late abated our establishment in many respects, in which our rank as a kingdom of the Union is in some degree compromised.

Last year a bill, deeply affecting the national

interests of Scotland, by altering many most important points in our judicature, was depending in Parliament. Grave objections appeared to the Law Bodies and others in Scotland, to attach to some particular arrangements thereby proposed. They required, not that the bill should be given up, but that it should be suspended at least, till the country in which it was to operate, and which alone was to be hurt or benefited by the enactment, should have time to consider the measure in all its bearings, and to express their national sense upon the subject. Can it be believed that it required the strongest possible remonstrances of the great Law-officer of the Crown with his Majesty's Ministers to obtain a few months' reprieve, as if the demolition, or alteration at least, of our laws, was a matter as little deserving a month's delay, as the execution of some flagrant criminal, justly and fully convicted of the most gross crimes? Take one or two instances more.

Till of late, there was always an Admiral on this station; but since the gallant Sir John Beresford struck his flag, that mark of distinction seems to have been laid aside, probably for ever

Our army establishment is dwindled to a shadow, scarce worthy of being placed under the command of the distinguished Major-General who now holds it, although he only commands the forces, instead of being, as was universally the case till of late years, a Commander-in-Chief, with a Lieutenant-General, and two Major-Generals, under him. I need hardly say, that I would wish this abatement of our dignity, in some measure at least, amended, not by the *removal*, but by the *promotion* of the gallant General.

It may be replied that we are complimented in being thus left to ourselves—that we are a moral people, therefore do not require a military force to keep the peace—a loyal people, therefore do not need an armed force to put down tumult—that we have our own brave yeomanry, who, at no distant period, showed themselves capable of affording their country protection in the most desirable manner, anticipating mischief by their promptitude, and preventing evil before it had come to a head. But have these yeomen, who twice in a few months abandoned their homes at a few hours' warning, marched many miles, and by their demonstration of readiness, put an end to a very serious affair, and what might have been a very disastrous one—have they, I say, since that period, received the countenance due for their good will from the Government, and which should have been rendered alike in policy and justice? I am informed that they have not. I am informed that they are, at least particular troops of them are, refused the small allowance made on the days when they are called out for exercise, and must either discharge the duty of training, always sufficiently expensive and inconvenient, entirely at their own expense, as some of them have done for two years, or suffer their discipline to fall into decay. Can it be that our English brethren have taken a notion that sabres are only curved broadswords, and that these are unhappy weapons in the hands of Scotsmen? I acquit them of such meanness. But they despise us a little too much.

Sir, Discontent is the child of Distress, and Distress is the daughter of ill-timed Experiment. Should we again see disorderly associations formed, and threats of open violence held out—should such a winter and spring as 1821

return, it may not, in the event of the measure
with which Scotland is threatened being inflicted on us, be quite so easy, as at that period, to
assemble on a given spot, within a day or two,
twelve or fourteen hundred yeomen to support
the handful of military left within Scotland.
That general spirit of loyalty will, I am sure,
be the same. But when proprietors are embar-
rassed, tenants distressed, commercial people in
doubt and danger, men lose at once their zeal,
and the means for serving the public. This is
not unworthy of serious consideration.

I mentioned in my former Letter another circumstance, of which I think my country has
reason to complain. It is that sort of absolute
and complete state of tutelage to which England seems disposed to reduce her sister country, subjecting her in all her relations to the
despotic authority of English Boards, which
exercise an exclusive jurisdiction in Scottish affairs, without regard to her local peculiarities,
and with something like contempt of her claims
as a country united with England, but which
certainly has never resigned the right of being
at least consulted in her own concerns. I men-

tioned the restrictions, and, as I conceive them, degrading incapacities, inflicted on our Revenue Boards,—I might extend the same observations to the regulations in the Stamp-Office ;—and I remember, when these were in progress, that it was said in good society, that the definitive instructions (verbal, I believe) communicated to the able officer upon whom the examination and adjustment of the alterations in that department devolved, and who was sent down hither on purpose, were to this purport :—" That he was to proceed in Scotland without more regard to the particular independence of that country than he would feel in Yorkshire." These, however, were matters interesting the general revenue—the servants of the Crown had a right to regulate them as they pleased. But if they were regulated with a purposed and obvious intention to lessen the consequence of Scotland, throw implied discredit on her natives, as men unworthy of trust, and hold her recollections and her feelings at nought, they make links in a chain which seems ready to be wound around us whenever our patience will permit.

This, sir, is an unwise, nay, an unsafe pro-

ceeding. An old chain, long worn, forms a cal-
losity on the limb which bears it, and is endured,
with whatever inconvenience, as a thing of custom. It is not so with restraints newly imposed.
These fret—gall—gangrene—the iron enters
first into the flesh, and then into the soul. I
speak out what more prudent men would keep
silent. I may lose friends by doing so; but he
who is like Malachi Malagrowther, old and un-
fortunate, has not many to lose, and risks little
in telling truths before, when men of rising am-
bition and budding hopes would leave them to
be discovered by the event.

But, besides such matters of punctilio, Mr
Journalist, there has been in England a gradual
and progressive system of assuming the management of affairs entirely and exclusively proper
to Scotland, as if we were totally unworthy of
having the management of our own concerns.
All must centre in London. We could not have
a Caledonian Canal, but the Commissioners must
be Englishmen, and meet in London;—a most
useful canal they would have made of it, had
not the lucky introduction of steam-boats—
—*Deus ex machina*—come just in time to re-

deem them from having made the most expensive and most useless undertaking of the kind ever heard of since Noah floated his ark ! We could not be intrusted with the charge of erecting our own kirks, (churches in the Highlands,) or of making our roads and bridges in the same wild districts, but these labours must be conducted under the tender care of men who knew nothing of our country, its wants and its capabilities, but who, nevertheless, sitting in their office in London, were to decide, without appeal, upon the conduct of the roads in Lochaber !—Good Heaven, sir ! to what are we fallen ?—or rather, what are we esteemed by the English ? Wretched drivellers, incapable of understanding our own affairs ; or greedy peculators, unfit to be trusted ? On what ground are we considered either as the one or the other ?

But I may perhaps be answered, that these operations are carried on by grants of public money ; and that, therefore, the English—undoubtedly the only disinterested and public-spirited and trust-worthy persons in the universe—must be empowered exclusively to look after its application. Public money forsooth !!!

I should like to know whose pocket it comes out of. Scotland, I have always heard, contributes FOUR MILLIONS to the public revenue. I should like to know, before we are twitted with grants of public money, how much of that income is dedicated to Scottish purposes—how much applied to the general uses of the empire—and if the balance should be found to a great amount on the side of Scotland, as I suspect it will, I should like still farther to know how the English are entitled to assume the direction and disposal of any pittance which may be permitted, out of the produce of our own burthens, to revert to the peculiar use of the nation from which it has been derived? If England was giving us alms, she would have a right to look after the administration of them, lest they should be misapplied or embezzled. If she is only consenting to afford us a small share of the revenue derived from our own kingdom, we have some title, methinks, to be consulted in the management, nay, intrusted with it.

This assumption of uncalled-for guardianship accelerates the circulation a little, and inclines one to say to his countrymen,

> Our blood has been too cold and temperate,
> Unapt to stir at such indignities———.

You could not keep a decent servant in your family, sir, far more a partner, if you obviously treated such a person as a man in whom no confidence was to be reposed even in his own department. We shall in due time, I suppose, be put all under English control, deprived even of the few native dignitaries and office-holders we have left, and accommodated with a set of English superintendants in every department. It will be upon the very reasoning of Goneril before alluded to :—

> " What need you five-and-twenty, ten, or five,
> To follow in a house where twice so many
> Have a command to tend you ?—"

Patrick, will you play Regan, and echo,

> "———What need *one ?*"

Take care, my good fellow ! for you will scarce get a great share in our spoils, and will be shortly incapacitated, and put under a statute of lunacy, as well as ourselves.

But what will England take by this engrossing spirit ? Not the miserable candle-ends and

cheese-parings—these, I dare say, she scorns.
The mere pleasure, then, of absolute authority
—the gratification of humour exacted by a peevish and petted child, who will not be contented
till he has the toy in his own hand, though he
break it the next moment.   Is any real power
derived by centering the immediate and direct
control of everything in London? Far from it.
On the contrary, that great metropolis is already a head too bulky for the empire, and,
should it take a vertigo, the limbs would be
unable to support it. The misfortune of France,
during the Revolution, in all its phases, was,
that no part of the kingdom could think for itself or act for itself; all were from habit neces-
sitated to look up to Paris.   Whoever was up-
permost there, and the worst party is apt to
prevail in a corrupted metropolis, were, without
possibility of effectual contradiction, the uncontrolled and despotic rulers of France—*absit
omen !*

Again, would the British empire become stronger, were it possible to annul and dissolve all the
distinctions and peculiarities, which, flowing out
of circumstances, historical events, and difference

of customs and climates, make its relative parts still, in some respects, three separate nations, though intimately incorporated into one empire? Every rope-maker knows, sir, that three distinct *strands*, as they are called, incorporated and twisted together, will make a cable ten times stronger than the same quantity of hemp, however artificially combined into a single twist of cord. The reason is obvious to the meanest capacity. If one of the strands happen to fail a little, there is a threefold chance that no imperfection will occur in the others at the same place, so that the infirm strand may give way a little, yet the whole cord remain trustworthy. If the single twist fail at any point, all is over. For God's sake, sir, let us remain as Nature made us, Englishmen, Irishmen, and Scotchmen, with something like the impress of our several countries upon each! We would not become better subjects, or more valuable members of the common empire, if we all resembled each other like so many smooth shillings. Let us love and cherish each other's virtues—bear with each other's failings—be tender to each other's prejudices—be scrupulously regardful of each other's rights.

Lastly, let us borrow each other's improvements, but never before they are needed and demanded. The degree of national diversity between different countries, is but an instance of that general variety which Nature seems to have ad *pted* as a principle through all her works, as ankious, apparently, to avoid, as modern statesmen to enforce, anything like an approach to aosolute " uniformity."

It may be said that some of the grievances I have complained of are mere trifles. I grant they are,—excepting in the feelings and intentions towards Scotland which they indicate. But, according to Bacon's maxim, you will see now the wind sits by flinging up a feather, which you cannot discern by throwing up a stone. Affronts are almost always more offensive than injuries, although they seldom are in themselves more than trifles. The omitting to discharge a gun or two in a salute, the raising or striking of a banner or sail, have been the source of bloody wars. England lost America about a few miserable chests of tea—she endangered India for the clipping of a mustachio.

But let us humble ourselves to our situation.

and confine our remonstrances to the immediate grievance, which surely cannot be termed punctilious or unimportant.

To England we say, therefore, Let us appeal from Philip intoxicated to Philip sober. Leave out exasperating circumstances on either side, and examine our remonstrance, not in the jealous feeling of which we have reason to complain, but in the gentlemanlike and liberal tone so much more becoming a great nation. and according, I must say, so much better with your natural disposition. As you mean that a value should be set upon your free public voice by your legislators, allow the natural influence of that of Scotland, in a matter exclusively relating to her own affairs, but so intimately connected with her welfare, that nothing since the year 1748 has occurred of such importance. The precedent is a bad one at any rate ; the consequences will be much worse.

> Prevent—resist it. Let it not be so,
> Lest children's children call against you—*woe !*

Our Scottish Nobles and Gentlemen, I canno better exhort to resist the proposal at every stage, by the most continued and unremitting opposition—to be discouraged by nothing—to hope to the last—to combat to the last—than by using once more the words of the patriotic Belhaver:—" Man's extremity is God's opportunity. He is a present help in time of need ; a deliverer, and that right early. Some unforeseen providence will fall out, that may cast the balance. Some Joseph will say, Why do you strive together when you are brethren ? Some Judah or other will say, Let not our hand be upon him, he is our brother. Let us up then, and be doing ; and let our noble patriots behave themselves like men, and we know not how soon a blessing may come."

I am, Mr Journalist,

Yours,

MALACHI MALAGROWTHER.

EDINBURGH:
Printed by James Ballantyne and Co.

A

THIRD LETTER

TO THE

Editor of the Edinburgh Weekly Journal,

FROM

MALACHI MALAGROWTHER, Esq.

ON THE

PROPOSED CHANGE OF CURRENCY,

AND

OTHER LATE ALTERATIONS,

AS THEY AFFECT, OR ARE INTENDED TO AFFECT,

THE

KINGDOM OF SCOTLAND

Macduff. Stands Scotland where it did ?
Rosse. Alas! poor country.

EDINBURGH :

Printed by James Ballantyne and Company,

FOR WILLIAM BLACKWOOD, EDINBURGH : AND

T. CADELL, STRAND, LONDON.

1826.

LETTER THIRD

ON THE

PROPOSED CHANGE OF CURRENCY.

———

TO THE EDITOR

OF THE EDINBURGH WEEKLY JOURNAL.

DEAR MR JOURNALIST,

THIS third set of Mr Baxter's last words is rather a trial on your patience, considering how much *Balaam* (speaking technically) I have edged out of your valuable paper; how I have trodden on the toes of your Domestic Intelligence, and pushed up to the wall even your Political Debates, until you have almost lost your honoured title of the EDINBURGH JOURNAL in that of MALACHI'S CHRONICLE.

I returned from the Meeting of Inhabitants on Friday last, sir, convoked for considering this question, with much feeling of gratification from what I saw and heard; but still a little disappointed that no one appeared on the opposite side, excepting one gentleman, ("self pulling," as Captain Crowe says, " against the whole ship's crew,") whose eloquence used no other argument than by recommending implicit deference to the wisdom of Ministers. I am a pretty stanch Tory myself, but not up to this point of humility. I never have nor will bargain for an implicit surrender of my private judgement in a national question of this sort. I am but an unit, but of units the whole sum of society is composed. On the present question, had I been the born servant of Ministers, I would have used to them the words of Cornwall's dependant, when he interferes to prevent his master from treading out Gloster's eyes—

> I have served you ever since I have been a child,
> But better service have I never done you,
> Than now to bid you *Hold*.

Or in a yet more spirited passage in the same drama—

> ———— Be Kent unmannerly,
> When Lear is mad.

To return to the business. By the unanimity of the meeting, I lost an opportunity of making a very smart extempore speech, which I had sate up half the night for the purpose of composing. To have so much eloquence die within me unuttered, excited feelings like those of Sancho, when, in the deserts of the Sierra Morena, his good things rotted in his gizzard. To console me, however, I found, on my return to my lodgings in the Lawn-market, my own lucubrations blazing in the goodly form of two responsible pamphlets. I seized on them as if I had never seen them before, and recited the more animated passages aloud, striding up and down a room, in which, from its dimensions, striding is not very convenient. I ended with reading aloud the motto, which I designed in the pride of my heart to prefix to my immortal twins, when, side by side, under the same comely cover, they shall travel down to posterity as a crown octavo ;—

> He set a bugle to his mouth,
>   And blew a blast sae shrill,
> The trees in greenwood shook thereat,
>   Sae loud rang ilka hill.

But while I mentally claimed for myself the honour of alarming Scotland, from Coldstream Bridge to the far Highlands, I was giving, by the noise I made, far greater alarm to my neighbour, Christopher Chrysal, who keeps the small hardware and miscellaneous shop under the turnpike stair.   Now, sir, you must know that Chrysal deals occasionally in broken tea-spoons and stray sugar-tongs, dismantled lockets and necklaces, (which have passed with more or less formality from ladies to their waiting-maids,) seals, out of which valets have knocked the stones that the setting might be rendered available, and such other small gear,—nay, I once saw an old silver coffee-pot in his possession. On the score, therefore, of being connected with the precious metals by his calling, neighbour Chrysal has set himself up for a patron and protector of Gold and Silver, and a stout contender for Bullion currency. With a half-crown in one hand, and a twenty-shilling note in the other, he will spout like a player over the two pictures in Hamlet, and it is great to hear him address them alternately—

Tʜɪs is the thing itself—Off, off, ye lendings!

But with all the contempt he expressed for the paper substitute, I have always seen that it steals quietly back to the solitude of his little pocket-book. Indeed, the barber says Mr Chrysal has other reasons for wishing a change of currency, or a currency of change, in respect of his own acceptances not being in these sharp times quite so locomotive as usual—They love the desk of the holder, sir, better than the counter of his great Neighbours in Bank Street. You under-stand me—but I hate scandal.

I had no sooner apologized to Christopher for the disturbance I had occasioned, (which I did with some shame of countenance,) than I polite-ly offered him a copy of my pamphlet. He thanked me, but added with a grin, (for you know no man is a prophet in his own common stair,) that he had nothing particular to wrap up at present : " But in troth, Mr Malachi," said he, " I looked over your pamphlet in the reading-room, and I must tell you as a friend, you have just made a fool of yourself, Mr Ma-lachi." " A fool!" replied I ; " when, how, and in what manner ?" " Ye have set out, sir," replied he,—for Chrysal is a kind of orator, and

speaks as scholarly and wisely as his neighbours,
—" with assuming the principle, which you
should have proved.—You say, that in consequence of restoring the healthful currency of the
precious metals, instead of keeping those ragged
scraps of paper, Scotland will experience a want
of the circulating medium, by which deprivation
her industry will be cramped, her manufactures
depressed, her fisheries destroyed, and so forth.
But you know nothing of the nature of the precious metals, and how should you ?"

" Why, not by dealing in old thimbles, broken buckles, and children's whistles, certainly, or
stolen *sprecherie*," said I ; " but speak out, man,
wherein do I evince ignorance of the nature of
the precious metals—tell me that ?"

" Why, Mr Malachi Malagrowther," said my
friend, in wrath, " I pronounce you ignorant of
the most ordinary principles of Political Economy. In your unadvised tract there, you have
shown yourself as irritable as Balaam, and as obstinate as his ass. You are making yourself and
other people fidgetty about the want of gold, to
supply the place of that snuff-paper of yours ;
now in this I repeat you are ignorant."

Here he raised his voice, as if speaking *ex cathedra*. " Gold," continued he, " is a commodity itself, though it be also the representative of other commodities ; just as a Banker is a man, though his business is to deal in money. Gold, therefore, like all other commodities, will flow to the place where there is a demand for it. It will be found, assure yourself, wherever it is most wanted ; just as, if you dig a well, water will percolate into it from all the neighbourhood. Twenty years ago you could not have seen a cigar in Edinburgh. Gillespie, the greatest snuff-merchant of his day, would not have known what you wanted had you asked him for one ; and now the shop-windows of the dealers are full of real Havannahs,—and why ?—because you see every writer's apprentice with a cigar in his mouth. It is the demand that makes the supply, and so it will be with the gold. The balance of free-trade, whether the commodity be gold or grain, will go where the one finds mouths to be fed, the other a currency to be supported. What sent specie into the lagoons of Venice, and into the swamps of Holland formerly, as well as into the emporium of London now, while

large cities, situated under a finer climate, and
in a more fertile country, were and are comparatively destitute of the precious metals?—what,
save the tendency of commerce, like water, to
find its own just level, and to send all the commodities subject to its influence, the precious
metals included, to the points where they are
most wanted ?"

Now, Mr Journalist, I am a man of a quick
temper, but somewhat of a slow wit; and though
it struck me that there was something fallacious
in this argument, yet, bolstered out as it was by
his favourite metaphor, it sounded so plausible,
that the right answer did not at once occur to
me. Chrysal went on in triumph : " You speak
of your Fisheries and Kelp manufacture, and
such like, and seem to dread that they will be
all ruined for want of a circulating medium.
But, sir, one of two things must happen. Either,
FIRST, assuming that these branches of industry
are beneficial to the individuals, and make advantageous returns ; as such they will have the
usual power of attracting towards them the
specie necessary to carry them on, and of course
no change whatever will take place. Or, SE-

CONDLY, these fisheries, and so forth, produce no adequate return for the labour expended on them, and are therefore a compulsory species of manufacture, like those establishments instituted at the direct expense, and under the immediate control of government, which we see fading in despotic countries, or only deriving a sickly existence by the expenditure of the Sovereign, and not by their own natural vigour. In that latter case," he pursued, " those fishing and kelping operations are not productive—are useless to the country—and ought not to be carried on an hour longer ; they only occasion the mis-employment of so much capital, the loss of so much labour. Leave your kelp-rocks to the undisturbed possession of seals and mermaids, if there be any—you will buy *barilla* cheaper in South America. Send your Highland fishers to America and Botany Bay, where they will find plenty of food, and let them leave their present sterile residence in the utter and undisturbed solitude for which Nature designed it. Do not think you do any hardship in obeying the universal law of nature, which leads wants and supplies to draw to their just and proper level, and equalize each other; which attracts gold to those spots, and those only, where it can be profitably employed, and induces man to transport himself from the realms of famine to those happier regions, where labour is light and subsistence plentiful.

"Lastly," said the unconscionable Christopher, "sweep out of your head, Mr Malachi, all that absurd rubbish of ancient tradition and history about national privileges—you might as well be angry with the Provost who pulled down the Lucken-booths. They do not belong to this day, in which so many changes have taken place, and so many more are to be expected. We look for what is USEFUL, sir, and to what is useful only; and our march towards utility is not to be interrupted by reference to antiquated treaties, or obsolete prejudices. So, while you sit flourishing your claymore, Mr Malachi, on the top of your Articles of Union, very like the figure of a Highlander on the sign of a whisky-office, take care you are not served as the giant who built his castle on the marvellous bean-stalk— Truth comes like the old woman with the ' cuttie-axe'—it costs but a swashing blow or two,

and down comes Malachi and his whole system."
—So saying, *exit* Christopher, *ovans.*

There was such a boldness and plausibility
about the fellow, and such a confidence in the
arguments which he expressed so fluently, that
I felt a temporary confusion of ideas, and was
obliged to throw myself into what has been, for
many generations, the considering position of
the Malagrowther family : that is to say, I flung
myself back in our hereditary easy-chair, fixing
my eyes on the roof, but keeping them, at the
same time, half shut ; having my hands folded,
and twirling my thumbs slowly around each
other, a motion highly useful in unravelling and
evolving the somewhat tangled thread of the
ideas. Thus seated, in something short of two
hours I succeeded in clearing out the ravelled
skean, which evolved itself in as orderly a coil
before me as if it had been touched by the rod
of Prince Percinet, in the fairy tale, and I am
about to communicate the result. I must needs
own that my discoveries went so far as was like
to have involved you in an examination of the
general principles on which the doctrine of currency depends. But since, *entre nous,* we might

get a little beyond our depth on the subject, I have restrained myself within the limits of the question, as practically applicable to Scotland.

My present business is to inquire how this meditated change of circulation, supposing it forcibly imposed on us, is to be accomplished—by what magic art, in other words, our paper is to be changed into gold, without some great national distress, nay, convulsion, *in transitu?*

My neighbour deems anxiety in this case quite ridiculous. Gold, he says, is a commodity, and whenever its presence becomes necessary, there it will appear. Guineas, according to Christopher, are like the fairy goblets in Parnell's tale,

——that with a wish come nigh,
And with a wish retire.

I don't know how it may be in national necessities, but I have some reason to think that friend Chrysal has not, any more than I have myself, found the maxim true, in so far as concerns our personal experience. I heartily wish, indeed, this comfortable doctrine extended to individual cases, and that the greater occasion a poor devil had for money, the more certain he should be of his wants being supplied by the arrival of that obliging article, which is said to come wherever it is wanted. Since Fortunatus's time, the contrary has in general proved to be the case, and I cannot deny it would be very convenient to us to have his system restored.

And yet there is some truth in what my neighbour says ; for if a man is indispensably obliged to have a sum of money, why he must make every effort to raise it. Supposing I was in business, and threatened with insolvency, I might find myself under the necessity of getting cash by selling property at an under rate, or procuring loans at usurious interet on what I retained, and in that ruinous manner I might raise money, because still nearer ruin stared me in the face if I did not. The question is, how long supplies so obtained could continue ?——Not an instant longer than I have articles to sell or to pawn. After this, my usual wants would be as pressing, but I might wish my heart out ere I found a groat to relieve them——No fairy will leave a silver penny in my shoe. Now I fear it must be by some such violent sacrifices, as those in the case supposed, that Scotland must purchase and maintain her metallic currency, if her present substitute is debarred.

Mr Chrysal's proposition should not then run, that gold will come when it is most needed, but should have been expressed thus,—that in countries where the presence of gold is rendered indispensable, it must be obtained, whatever price is given for it, while the means of paying such a price remain.

He amuses himself, indeed, and puzzles his hearers, by affirming that gold is like water, and, like water when poured out, it will find its level.—A metaphor is no argument in any instance ; but I think I can contrive in the present to turn my friend's own water-engine against him. Scotland, sir, is not *beneath* the level to which gold flows naturally. She is *above* that level, and she may perish for want of it ere she sees a guinea, without she, or the State for her, be at the perpetual expense of maintaining, by constant expenditure of a large per centage, that metallic currency which has a natural tendency to escape from a poor country back to a rich one. Just so, a man might die of thirst on the top of a Scottish hill, though a river or a lake lay at the base of it. Therefore, if we insist upon the favourite comparison of gold to water, we must conceive the possibility of the golden Pactolus flowing up Glencroe in an opposite direction to the natural element, which trots down from the celebrated *Rest and be Thankful*.

If my friend would consult the clerk of the Water Company, at his office in the Royal Exchange, he would explain the matter at once. " Let me have," says Mr Chrysal, " a pipe of water to my house."—" Certainly, sir ; it will cost you forty shillings yearly."—" The devil it will ! Why, surely the Lawnmarket is lower than the Reservoir on the Castlehill ? It is the nature of water to come to a level. What title have you to charge me money, when the element is only obeying the laws of Nature, and descending to its level ?"—" Very true, sir," replies the clerk ; " but then it was no law of Nature brought it to the reservoir, at a height which was necessary to enable us to disperse the supply over the city. On the contrary, it was an exertion of Art in despite of Nature. It was forced hither by much labour and ingenuity. Lakes were formed, aqueducts constructed, rivers dammed up, pipes laid for many miles. Without immense expense, the water could never have been brought here ; and without your paying a rateable charge, you cannot have the benefit of it."

This is exactly the case with the gold currency. It must have a natural tendency to centre in London, for the exchange is heavily against Scotland. We have the whole public income, four millions a-year, to remit thither. Independent of that large and copious drain, we have occasion to send to England the rents of non-resident proprietors, and a thousand other payments to make to London, which must be done in specie, or by bills payable in the metropolis. So that the circulation moves thither of free will, like a horse led by the bridle ; while Scotland's attempts to detain it, are like those of a wild Highlandman catching his pony by the tail. Or, to take a very old comparison, London is like Aboulcasem's well, full of gold, gems, and everything valuable. The rich contents are drawn from it by operations resembling those of a forcing-pump, which compel small portions into the extreme corners of the kingdom ; but all these golden streamlets, when left to themselves, trickle back to the main reservoir.

My friend's idea of a voluntary, unsolicited, and unbought supply of metallic currency, is like the reasoning of old Merrythought, when, with only a shilling in his pocket, he expresses a resolution to continue a jovial course of life. " But how wilt thou come by the means, Charles ?" says his wife. " How ?" replied the gay old gentleman, in a full reliance on his resources,—" How ?—Why, how have I done hitherto, these forty years ?—I never came into my dining-room, but, at eleven and six o'clock, I found excellent meat and drink on the table. My clothes were never worn out, but next morning a tailor brought me a new suit, and, without question, it will be so ever—use makes perfectness." The dramatist has rescued his jolly epicurean out of the scrape before his slender stock was exhausted ; but in what mode Scotland is to be relieved from the expense about to be imposed on a country, where industry and skill can but play a saving game, at best, against national disadvantages, is not so easy to imagine.

What may be the expense of purchasing in the outset, and maintaining in constant supply, a million and a half of gold, I cannot pretend to calculate, but something may be guessed from the following items :—To begin, like Mrs Glass's recipe for dressing a hare, *first catch your hare* —first buy your gold at whatever sacrifice of loss of exchange ; then add to the price a reasonable profit to those who are to advance the purchase-money—next insure your specie against water-thieves and land-thieves, peril of winds, waves, and rocks, from the Mint to the wharf, from the wharf to Leith, from Leith to Edinburgh, from Edinburgh to the most remote parts of Scotland, unprotected by police of any kind—the insurances can be no trifle ; besides, that an accident or two, like the loss of the Delight smack the other day, with L.4000 of specie on board, will make a tolerably heavy addition to other bills of charges, as the expense of carriages, guards, and so forth—then add the items together, and compute the dead loss of interest upon the whole sum. The whole may be moderately calculated at an expense of more than *five per cent*, a charge which must ultimately be laid on the Scottish manufactures, agricultural operations, fisheries, and other public and private undertakings; many of which are not at present returning twelve or fifteen per cent of profit at the uttermost.

My friend Chrysal's reasoning rested on this great mistake, that he confounds the necessity of our procuring gold under the operation of the new system, and the supplies which that necessity must necessarily oblige us to purchase, with a voluntary determination of unbought treasures running up-hill to find their level at Stornoway, Tongue, or Oban. He imagines that the specie, for which we have to pay a heavy consideration, will come to our service voluntarily. I answer, in one word, the gold will come, if purchased, AND NOT OTHERWISE. The expense attending the operation will be just a tax upon the parties who pay it, with this difference, that it makes no addition to the public revenue. Every sovereign we get, which passes of course for twenty shillings, will, before it gets to the north of Scotland, have cost *one*-and-twenty. Illustrations of so plain a proposition are endless. Suppose Government had imposed a stamp-duty upon any commodity, and, whilst with some other cowl'd neighbours I am canvassing its effects, I ask, as a party concerned,—" But how are we to come by these stamps ? The branch of commerce to which they apply is not able to bear the impost." Up rises my friend Chrysal in reply—" Stamped paper," says he, " is a commodity ; and, like all commodities, flows to the point where there is a demand." True—but, unhappily, when the stamp-paper is in bodily presence, I cannot have a slip of it till I pay the impost ; and if my trade does not enable me to do so, I must give it up, or be a ruined man !

The same consequences must attend the increased expense of the circulation under the proposed measure, as would apply to a tax in any other form. The manufactures, public works, and private speculations, which are making a return, enabling them to defray the charge attending the more expensive medium of circulation, will struggle on as they can, with less profit by the direct amount, and more disadvantages arising from the means of circulation being at the mercy of winds and waves, and subjected to long and perilous transportation before the gold reaches them. Those, on the other hand, whose trade makes more precarious returns, will be no longer able to wait for better times. They will give up all, and the consequences to Scotland—and England also—omitting all allusion to individual distress, will be a black history.

I have already said, that the Fisheries and Kelp shores, and improvements on the more bleak and distant districts, will probably be the first sufferers. And my neighbour replies, with a sweeping argument, that enterprises which cannot support themselves by their own exertions, and natural returns of profit, ought not to have the encouragement of Government— that they are only vain schemes, in which labour and expense are wasted without their bringing the necessary return, and that the force employed in keeping up these barren and fruitless undertakings should, as soon as possible, be directed into a more productive channel. If I urge, that, although these undertakings may not, as yet, have made the full returns expected, yet they support many people, natives of a country otherwise too poor to furnish the means of livelihood to its inhabitants,—why, the answer is equally ready. Let the High-

lander emigrate, or be transported to Botany
Bay; and supply his place with sheep,—goats,
—anything,—or nothing at all.

I do not mean to deny, sir, that there is general truth in the maxims, which recommend
that a free trade be left to sustain itself by its
own exertions; deprecating the system of forcing commerce when its natural efforts were
not successful, and warning against planting
colonies in unhealthy or barren spots, where
the colonists must perish, or exist in a state of
miserable and precarious dependence on the
bounties of the mother country. To these political truths I subscribe cheerfully.—But an
old civilian used to tell me, *fraus latet in gene-
ralibus;* and no general maxim can be safely,
wisely, or justly applied, until it has been care-
fully considered how far it is controlled by the
peculiar circumstances of the case. The precepts of Religion herself, as expressed in the
holiest texts of Scripture, have been wrested
into sophistry—the soundest political principles
may, by the frigid subtleties of metaphysical
moonshine, be extended so as, in appearance, to
authorise aggressions on national rights, as well

as on the dictates of sound wisdom and humanity.

I have more replies than one to my neighbour's doctrines of Political Economy, (though true in the abstract,) when I consider them as applicable to the case in question.

In the *first* place, I deny that the Scottish Fisheries are in the predicament to which the maxim, quoted triumphantly by my friend Chrysal, applies. I say that they are already supporting themselves, and producing a moderate but certain profit; only that this profit is as yet *so* moderate, that it certainly will not bear an impost of probably five or six per cent upon the gross capital employed; and that, therefore, it is the highest impolicy to smother, by such a burthen, important national undertakings, which are, without such new imposition, in a condition to maintain themselves. It would be breaking the reed ere it had attained its strength, and quenching the smoking flax just when about to burst into flame.

Secondly, Admitting, from the great poverty of the inhabitants, and other discouraging circumstances, that the Scottish fisheries have for a long time required the support of Government, I still aver, that the expense attending such support has been well and wisely disposed of,—just as a landlord would act not generously only, but most prudently, in giving favourable terms of settlement to a tenant, who was to improve his farm largely. An exotic shrub, when first planted, must be watered and cared for—a child requires tenderness and indulgence till he has got through the sickly and helpless years of infancy. A fishery or manufacture, established in a wild country, and among a population of indolent habits, unaccustomed to industry, and to the enjoyment of the profits derived from it, will at the outset require assistance from the State, till old habits are surmounted, and difficulties overcome. There is something in the nature of the people, who have been long depressed by poverty, resembling the qualities of their own peat-earth. Left alone, it is the most anti-septic and inert of Nature's productions; but when, according to the process of compost invented by the late ingenious Lord Meadowbank, this *caput mortuum* is intermixed with a small portion of active manure, it heats, ferments, changes its sluggish nature, and fertilizes the whole country in the vicinity. No agriculturist regards the expense of the proportion of manure necessary to commence this vivifying operation; and neither will any wise government regret the outlay of sums employed in exciting the industry, improving the comforts, and amending the condition, of its inhabitants. In the present case, Government has done this duty amply—The tree has taken root, the child is rising fast to youth and manhood—the establishments of the fisheries are in full progress to triumphant success. The question is not, if you are yet to continue your encouragement—nor whether the public is to save some expense by withdrawing it. In these questions there would be a direct and palpable motive, that of a saving to the State, which, so far as it went, would be a real, if not an adequate motive, for breaking up these establishments. But the question at issue turns on this very different point—whether, by a measure obnoxious to Scotland, and in which England cannot challenge an interest remote or direct, you are to adopt an enactment so likely to create the ruin of these establishments, now that they have already attained prosperity? The wish of many of the wisest English patriots has been accomplished—the barren and desolate shores are compensated in that desolation by the riches of the sea—foreigners are driven from engrossing as formerly their wealth, and selling to Britain herself, at advantage, the produce of her own coasts. Thriving villages are already found where there were scarcely to be seen the most wretched hovels ; a population lazy and indolent, because they had no motive for exertion, have become, on finding the employment, and tasting the fruits of industry, an enterprizing and hardy race of seamen, well qualified to enrich their country in peace—to defend her in time of war. *All this* is GAINED. Shall all be lost again, to render the system of currency betwixt England and Scotland uniform ? all sacrificed to what I can call little more than a political conundrum ? In my opinion, the Dutchmen might as well cut the dikes, and let the sea in upon the land their industry has gained from it. In the case of Holland, she would at least save the money expended in maintaining her ramparts. In our case, the state gains nothing and loses everything.

Lastly, I would say a word in behalf of the people of Scotland, merely as human beings, and entitled to consideration as such. I will suppose this alteration is recommended by some expected advantages of great importance, but the nature of which are prudently concealed. I will suppose, what is not easily understood, that in some unintelligible manner England is to gain with addition what Scotland is condemned to lose. (The process, by the way, seems to resemble that recommended by Moliere's quack, who prescribes the putting out of one eye, that the other may see further, and more acutely.) I will suppose that our statesmen, by enforcing this measure, condemn to emigration, or transportation —the punishment she inflicts on felons—the inhabitants of distant and desert tracts, on the mainland and in the Hebrides, to save her from some expense, and because she thinks a country so different from her own fertile valleys, cannot be fit for human habitation. In that case, I would say, Consider, first, the character of the population you are about to consign thus summarily to the effects which must follow the destroying their present means of livelihood. My countrymen have their faults, and I am well aware of them. But this I will say, that there is more vice, more crime—nay, more real want and misery, more degrading pauperism and irremediable wretchedness, in the parish of Saint Giles's alone, than in the whole Highlands and pastoral districts of Scotland, or perhaps in all Scotland together. Poor as the inhabitants are, the wants of the Highlanders are limited to their circumstances ; and they have enjoyments which make amends, in their own way of reckoning, for deprivations which they do not greatly feel. Their land is to them a land of many recollections. I will not dwell on that subject, lest I be thought fantastic in harping on a tune so obsolete. But every heart must feel some sympathy when I say, they love their country, rude as it is, because it holds the churches where their fathers worshipped, and the churchyards where their bones are laid.

This is not all. Mountainous countries inspire peculiarly strong attachments into the natives, showing perhaps, if we argue up to the Final Great Cause, that while it was the pleasure of God that men should exist in all parts of the world, which His pleasure called into being, the Beneficence of the Common Father annexed circumstances of consolation, which should compensate the mountaineers for want of the fertility and fine climate enjoyed by the inhabitants of the plain. Some philosophers, looking to secondary causes, have referred the sense of this local attachment amongst mountaineers to the influence of the sublime though desolate scenery around them, as stamping the idea of a peculiar country more deeply on their bosoms. The chief cause seems to me to be, that such tribes rarely change their dwellings, and therefore become more wedded to their native districts than are the inhabitants of those where the population is frequently fluctuating. The land is not only theirs *now*, it pertained to a long list of fathers before them ; and the coldest philosopher will regard what is called a family estate with greater attachment than he applies to a recent purchase.

But independent of this, the inhabitants of

the wilder districts in Scotland have actually some enjoyments, both moral and physical, which compensate for the want of better subsistence and more comfortable lodging. In a word, they have more liberty than the inhabitants of the richer soil. Englishmen will start at this as a paradox; but it is very true notwithstanding, that if one great privilege of liberty be the power of going where a man pleases, the Scotch peasant enjoys it much more than the English. The pleasure of viewing " fair Nature's face," and a great many other primitive enjoyments, for which a better diet and lodging are but indifferent substitutes, are more within the power of the poor man in Scotland than in the sister country. A Scottish gentleman, in the wilder districts, is seldom severe in excluding his poor neighbours from his grounds; and I have known many that have voluntarily thrown them open to all quiet and decent persons who wish to enjoy them. The game of such liberal proprietors, their plantations, their fences, and all that is apt to suffer from intruders, have, I have observed, been better protected than where

severer measures of general seclusion were adopted. *Haud inexpertus loquor.*

But in many districts, the part of the soil
which, with the utmost stretch of appropriation,
the first-born of Egypt can set apart for his own
exclusive use, bears a small proportion indeed
to the uncultivated wastes. The step of the
mountaineer on his wild heath, solitary mountain, and beside his far-spread lake, is more free
than that which is confined to a dusty turnpike,
and warned from casual deviation by advertise-
ments which menace the summary vindication
of the proprietor's monopoly of his extensive
park, by spring-guns or man-traps, or the more
protracted, yet scarce less formidable denun-
ciation, of what is often, and scarce unjustly
spelled, " *persecution* according to law." Above
all, the peasant lives and dies as his fathers did,
in the cot where he was born, without ever ex-
periencing the horrors of a work-house. This
may compensate for the want of much beef,
beer, and pudding, in those to whom habit has
not made this diet indispensable.

It is to be hoped that experimental legislation
will pause ere consigning a race which is con-

tented with its situation to banishment, because they only offer at present their hardy virtues and industry to the stock of national prosperity, instead of communicating largely to national wealth. Even considered as absolute paupers, they have some right to such slight support as may be necessary to aid them in maintaining themselves by their own industry. If the poor elsewhere could be maintained without the degrading sense that they were receiving eleemosynary aid, it would be the better for themselves and their country.

I will admit, for argument's sake, that the public funds which have established those fishing stations might have been bestowed to better advantage; still, having been so expended, we ought certainly not to be hasty in withdrawing our support, even if we may judge that it was incautiously granted at first. The philosopher, in the fanciful Tale of Frankenstein, acted unwisely in creating the unnatural being to which art enabled him to give life and motion; but when he had, like a second Prometheus, given sensation and power of thought to the creation of his skill and science, he had no title to desert

the giant whom he had called into existence ;
and the story shows that no good came of his
being discontented with his own handy-work.
But I contend, that the establishments to which
I allude exhibit nothing save what may render
the founders and encouragers proud of the result of their patriotic labours.

I do therefore hope that the present contented and rapidly improving condition of so many
fellow-creatures, will be considered as something
in the scale, when a measure shall be finally
weighed, which, in the opinion of all connected
with the north of Scotland, threatens to deprive
them of the means of livelihood.

On other national topics I have already said
enough. Those who look only at states and
ledgers, hold such feelings as arise upon points
of national honour, as valueless as a cypher
without a numeral prefixed. Right or wrong,
however, they still have an effect on the people
of Scotland, as all can bear witness who were
here when his Majesty honoured the capital of
his ancestors with his own presence. We would
not plead these too high neither, nor cling tena-
ciously by antiquated pretensions, which may

obstruct the general welfare of the empire ; but we deprecate that sort of change which is made for the mere sake of innovation. A proud nation cannot endure such experiments when they touch honour—a poor one cannot brook them when attended with heavy loss. We are all aware that many changes must of necessity be —the political atmosphere is heavy and gloomy with the symptoms of them,

" And coming events cast their shadows before."

These changes will be wrought in their time ; but we trust they will not be forced forward suddenly, or until the public mind is prepared for, and the circumstances of the country require them.

Seasonable improvements are like the timely and regular showers, which, falling softly and silently upon the earth, when fittest to be received, awaken its powers of fertility. Hasty innovation is like the headlong hurricane, which may indeed be ultimately followed by beneficial consequences, but is, in its commencement and immediate progress, attended by terror, tumult, and distress.

This is indeed a period when change of every kind is boldly urged and ingeniously supported, nay, finds support in its very singularity; as the wildest doctrines of enthusiasm have been often pleaded with most eloquence, and adopted with most zeal. One philosopher will convert the whole country into work-houses, just as Commodore Trunnion would have arranged each parish on the system of a man-of-war. Another class has turned the system of Ethics out of doors, and discovers on the exterior of the scull, the passions of which we used to look for the source within. One set of fanatics join to dethrone the Deity, another to set up Prince Hohenloe. The supporters of all find preachers, hearers, and zealots, and would find martyrs if persecuted. We are at such a speculative period obliged to be cautious in adopting measures which are supported only by speculative argument. Let men reason as ingeniously as they will, and we will listen to them, amused if we are not convinced. I have heard with great pleasure an ingenious person lecture on phrenology, and have been much interested in his process of reasoning. But should such a philosopher propose to saw off or file away any of the bumps on my scull, by way of improving the moral sense, I am afraid I should demur to the motion.

I have read, I think in Lucian, of two architects, who contended before the people at Athens which should be intrusted with the task of erecting a temple.   The first made a luminous oration, showing that he was, in theory at least, master of his art, and spoke with such glibness in the hard terms of architecture, that the assembly could scarce be prevailed on to listen to his opponent, an old man of unpretending appearance,   But when he obtained audience, he said in a few words, " All that this young man can talk of, I have DONE."   The decision was unanimously in favour of Experience against Theory.   This resembles exactly the question now tried before us.

Here stands Theory, a scroll in her hand, full of deep and mysterious combinations of figures, the least failure in any one of which may alter the result entirely, and which you must take on trust, for who is capable to go through and check them ? *There* lies before you a practical

System, successful for upwards of a century. The one allures you with promises, as the saying goes, of untold gold,—the other appeals to the miracles already wrought in your behalf. The one shows you provinces, the wealth of which has been tripled under her management, —the other a problem which has never been practically solved. Here you have a pamphlet —there a fishing town—here the long-continued prosperity of a whole nation—and there the opinion of a professor of Economics, that in such circumstances she ought not by true principles to have prospered at all. In short, good countrymen, if you are determined, like Æsop's dog, to snap at the shadow and lose the substance, you had never such a gratuitous opportunity of exchanging food and wealth for moonshine in the water.

Adieu, sir. This is the last letter you will receive from,

Yours, &c.

MALACHI MALAGROWTHER.

EDINBURGH:
Printed by James Ballantyne & Co.

TWO LETTERS

TO

MALACHI MALAGROWTHER, Esq.

TWO LETTERS

ON

SCOTTISH AFFAIRS,

FROM

EDWARD BRADWARDINE WAVERLEY, Esq.

TO

MALACHI MALAGROWTHER, Esq.,

" I believe I have satisfied you, Colonel Mac Ivor, that your resentment was founded on a misapprehension.—You must state this matter
properly to your Clan, to prevent a recurrence of their precipitate
violence."——WAVERLEY.

LONDON:

JOHN MURRAY, ALBEMARLE STREET;

AND

OLIVER AND BOYD, EDINBURGH.

MDCCCXXVI.

LONDON:
PRINTED BY WILLIAM CLOWES,
Northumberland-court.

MALACHI MALAGROWTHER, Esq.

Waverley-Honour, Feb. 28, 1826.

MY DEAR COUSIN,

Distant as our relationship is, I can never hesitate to acknowledge it, out of respect to that illustrious person whom fame reports to be our common progenitor.

I thank you for sending me a copy of your Pamphlet on the " Proposed Change of the Currency in Scotland," and I hope you will take in good part the criticism which I cannot, I own, repress on this production.

I never can cease to feel a deep interest in every thing that relates to Scotland. I have Scotch blood in my veins, derived from my grandmother, the celebrated Rose Bradwardine; and, by the increase of manufactures and the im-

provements of agriculture, the estate of Tully
Veolan, which I derive from her, gives me a still
more substantial claim to concern myself in
Scottish affairs.

I therefore need, I hope, make no apology for
the following observations, which, as a *Briton*,
deriving my blood from the Caledonians and the
Saxons, and possessing property both in Scotland and England, I think myself not merely
justified, but, in honour and conscience, obliged
to make.

I need not tell *you* that the remoteness of our
relationship, and of our residence (to say nothing
of *principles*) has precluded any acquaintance between me and the Malagrowthers ; but I confess
that I am surprised, as well as concerned, to find
in you so little resemblance to our common
parent.

He was not only one of the ablest men of his
day in all the walks of literature, but he sweetened even the bitter cup of politics with candour
and good humour, and, in all the ordinary inter-
courses of life, was cheerful, friendly, right-
headed, and, above all, right-hearted. You, on
the contrary, make it your boast that you are

poor and peevish—a growler by profession—one
who suffers under a chronic jaundice—and I fear
that, in addition to the amiable picture which you
thus draw of yourself, it may be shown that your
reasoning is no better than your temper, and that,
to borrow poor Sheridan's elaborate sarcasm,
you draw on your fancy for your facts, and on
your memory for your jokes.

It is not the least proof of how much you de-
generate from the good taste of your illustrious
progenitor, that you have thought the peevish-
ness, which might be excused in the hasty co-
lumns of a newspaper, worth preserving in the
more permanent shape of a pamphlet.

It is to this pamphlet that I mean to apply my
observations; and I shall begin with its title-
page, for I think you have fallen into the ominous misfortune of stumbling at the threshold.

The object of your pamphlet is, as this title-
page informs us, to complain of the " Proposed
change of Currency, and other late alterations, as
they affect, or are intended to affect, the *Kingdom of Scotland;*" and, in the course of your
letter, you ridicule and revile all such alterations
as either silly or insulting attempts to establish

a system of *assimilation and uniformity* in law, revenue, and commercial finance, between Scotland and England.

Now, my dear Sir, this too-candid title page advances a radical error, which pervades your whole letter—*the kingdom of Scotland!* If Scotland were indeed a *kingdom*—a separate and independent sovereignty—the question of uniformity and assimilation might be open to *some*, though certainly not to *all*, the observations you make, but, as the case happens to be, you have mistaken *Sister Peg* (as you elsewhere are pleased to designate her) for QUEEN *Margaret;* and your prognostics, allow me to say, are just of the same force as the opinion of the Empiric, who, having been consulted (in that peculiar mode which was the fashion of his day) on a case which he supposed to be that of a Lady, was so unlucky as to pronounce that a Doctor of Divinity was pregnant, and to prescribe for the reverend gentleman certain means and medicaments, altogether unsuitable to the real state of the affair.

You mention in your letter, that you had heard from your grandfather, of a certain old treaty,

called the Treaty of Union, and you profess a
hope that this obsolete document may even yet
be discovered and exhibited in the Museum of
Scottish Antiquities.

You need scarcely have told us, that you had
never seen this treaty. Every page of your
letter, from the title to the colophon, exhibits a
happy ignorance both of its enactments and its
spirit, but as I have had the good fortune to
meet with a copy of this recondite document, I
can take upon myself to inform you, that, some-
where about the year 1707, Scotland ceased to
be a *kingdom*, as also did England, and the separate nationalities of each were merged in the Imperial name and sovereignty of Great Britain;
and I think that your idea of a UNION, which was
not to lead to assimilation of laws and manners
and to identity of feelings and interests, might
be expected to have occurred to the blundering
brains of Paddy Blake, rather than to the pre-
cise and dialectic frame of mind to which the
Malagrowthers lay claim.

In most *unions* the bride is expected to assume
the name, share the fortunes, and assimilate
with the manners, of the husband. Your notion

of what was to be expected from Scotland, on
her union with England, seems on the contrary,
to be like that which your renowned relative,
Sir Mungo, entertained of Mrs. Martha Trap-
bois, when she condescended to intermarry with
Mr. Ritchie Moniplies. " It seems to me," said
the knight, " that this bride of yours is like to
be *master* and *mair* in the conjugal state."

To this little error of your title-page, relative
to the KINGDOM of Scotland, you subjoin a scrap
of Latin not much more fortunate—

Ergo, Caledonia, nomen inane, vale !

By this motto you must, I suppose, mean that
the late and present measures of the Goverment
have reduced your *kingdom* of Scotland to the
state of pitiable desertion which that quotation
implies.

Now, as the quotation seems to be of no
very modern date (though it certainly does not
belong to *classical* times), it follows that Ministers, according to your own shewing, are only
bringing back Scotland to her pristine state;
and you must also admit that nothing has been,
in past times, more frequent than a Scotch-

man's bidding farewell to his country—"*Inani-*
tatis ergo." So far, at least, no *laudator tempo-*
ris acti could have any reason to complain, even
if the quotation were apposite ; but I am justified
in adding that some of the very measures against
which you remonstrate, have tended very much to
produce a happier state of things—to substitute
wealth and plenty for the said inanity, and the
power of living comfortably at home, to the necessity of bidding " *farewell to Caledonia !*"

I have dwelt a little longer on your title-page
than perhaps might have been expected ; but I
am a literary physiognomist, and I thought I
saw in the features of your frontispiece, strong
characteristics of what was to follow.

I shall now proceed to observe on the succes-
sive points of your letter itself.

You begin by complaining of alterations of the
LAW, and you expend ten pages in condemning
all such innovations in the lump. You complain
that the English, so averse to any inroad on their
own habits, are yet willing enough to impose
them on their neighbours, and " that, *like the*
" *Friars in the Duenna*, the English Monks of the
" law will not tolerate in their lay brethren of the

" North" the same feeling of respect and attachment to their legal institutions which the English
entertain for theirs.

I do not exactly see the drift of this allusion.
In the *Duenna*, if I recollect aright, the Monks
denied to the lay brother a participation in their
luxury, whereas your meaning seems to be, that
the perverse generosity of the English endeavours
to cram these good things down the throats of
the reluctant Scotch.   The illustration must, I
think, be admitted to be a blunder.

You are very grateful that this spirit of innovation was not applied to Scotland for the first
fifty years of the last century; but you are grateful, not so much to the Ministers and Statesmen
of those days, as to the " *edges of the Scotch claymores*," to which—with rather less loyalty than
belongs to our family—you are pleased to
allude.

I shall not stop to inquire whether the *edge of
a claymore* is a good argument in a question of
legal improvement or civil administration, nor
will I insist on the obvious retort that, if *claymores*
had *edges* at Preston-Pans, *bayonets* had *points*
at Culloden ; but I will say, that if you meant to

excite our sympathy, and to conciliate our good will, towards Scotland, you take a strange mode of doing so by re 1 inding us of h(r rebellions, at once so absurd and so atrocious, and by referring, *as the chosen and regretted period of national happiness*, to those fifty years, during which Scotland was, in the opinion of all mankind (except the Malagrowthers), impoverished and disgraced by disaffection and political bigotry, by tumults against the laws, and by insurrections against the liberties of the land.

But allow me to acquaint you, that your *minatory* allusion is historically false ; for in the year 1725, just in the middle of that period in which you think your claymores were so influential, one of the first, the greatest, and the most offensive, of our modern innovations, was effected by the Act for Disarming the Highlands.

—This Act, I admit, shewed that we thought your claymores dangerous implements, but it shewed, also, that they did not deter the Imperial Parliament from doing its duty by Scotland and by the Empire.

But if, in your opinion, the claymores saved your beloved country from innovation during the first half century, *contempt*, you say, secured her during the last.

"Neglected as she was, and perhaps because "she was neglected, Scotland, *during the space* "*from the close of the American War* TO THE PRE-"SENT DAY, has increased her prosperity in a "ratio *more than five times greater* than that of "England."

Such are your own words, such is your unequivocal admission;—*down to the present day too ! ! !* Scotland has gone on improving, in a five-fold ratio, for *fifty* years, *down to the present day*, and yet the first part of your letter is full of *complaints* of innovations made within the last five-and-twenty years; and I will add, what you omit, that, *during the whole of that period*, innovations have been gradually, but steadily, in progress. No year has passed without some moral approximation of Scotland and England, and the result is—National degradation?—Public distress?—Retrogradation in wealth, happiness, and honour?—No—but a FIVE-FOLD *increase in every species of prosperity!*

You are a cynical creature, Malachi, but your disposition to *truth* is stronger even than your bile, and forces itself through the melancholy mist in which a fit of ill humour has shrouded your intellect.

Again—after denouncing all the alterations which, during the last 20 years, have taken place in the law in Scotland as " *the wanton inroads of every juvenile statesman*"—as the " *manglings of junior students in a common dissecting room*"—as, in short, " *experimenta in corpore vili* "—you, the very next moment, like a vicious cow, kick down your own pail, and, with the same inconsistent candour which I have just remarked upon, you proceed to contradict, even in terms, every syllable you have written.

" I do not mean to dispute," you say, " that " *much alteration* was NECESSARY in our laws, and " that much benefit has followed many of the " great changes which have taken place; I do not " mean to deprecate a gradual approach to the " English system, especially in commercial law. " The Jury Court, for example, was a fair " experiment, in my opinion, cautiously intro- " duced as such, and placed under such regula- " tions as might best assimilate its forms with " those of the existing Supreme Court."

Could there be, I ask—supposing Malachi Malagrowther to be a person of some authority—could there be a more direct approval of what had been done, or a stronger encouragement to proceed in so *beneficial a course*, than the above quoted sentence affords?

I could have wished indeed, that your approbation had been more frank and generous, less alloyed by peevish reserves, and captious exceptions, and that your view of the gradual improvements of Scotland had partaken more of the candid and liberal spirit of Baillie Nicol Jarvie, than the narrow prejudices of Andrew Fairservice. I cannot resist the pleasure of quoting the passage in which the magic pen of our family historian has contrasted the sentiments of those characters.

" The Baillie saw with the prospective eye of
" an enlightened patriot, the buds of many of
" those future advantages which have only *blos-*
" *somed* and *ripened within these few years.* I
" remarked also, and with great pleasure, that
" although a keen Scotchman, and abundantly
" zealous for the honor of his country, he was
" disposed to think liberally of the sister king-

" dom. When Andrew Fairservice (whom, by the
" way, the Baillie could not abide) chose to im-
" pute the accident of one of the horses casting his
" shoe to the deteriorating influence of the *Union*,
" he incurred a severe rebuke from Mr. Jarvie*."

This passage seems very " germain to the
matter " in discussion between us. Our historian,
you see, does not agree with you that the last few
years have been marked with any thing disho-
nourable or disadvantageous to Scotland : on the
contrary, he says, that in them your prosperity,
which was only *in bud* before, has *blossomed* and
ripened. I recommend also to your observation
the liberal and grateful spirit in which Mr. Jarvie
was disposed to receive the interference of England; and I think that if you had had in your memory Mr. Fairservice's ludicrous appeal to the
Union, on the subject of the horse-shoe, you would
not have invoked the spirit of that solemn treaty,
on the matter of the dismissal of an exciseman.

But, even when you are obliged to admit
that the *measures* themselves have been right
and beneficial, you complain that they were
not introduced by the *proper persons*. You

* Rob Roy, Vol. ii. p. 310.

confess that the haggis is excellent, and the cock-a-leekie as good, as that of which King James and Sir Mungo partook at Castle-Collop* ; but it quite turns your stomach to think that they were not prepared by a genuine Scotch cook. Such nicety, methinks " savours of affectations," and, if the fact were true, it would rather be complimentary to those who had studied the Scotch palate with such nice discrimination and such complete success; but I take leave to inform you that your fact is unfounded. As you affect never to have seen the Treaty of Union, it is probable that you have no great acquaintance with the Statute Book, and I shall, therefore, not refer you to a volume, more formidable than that of the *wizard Scott ;* but there are some less recondite sources of information to which I may venture to allude.

I have now before me, in the *Edinburgh Annual Register* of 1808, an essay, entitled " A View of the changes proposed and adopted in the administration of justice in Scotland." This paper has been attributed to our excellent friend *Sir Walter Scott,* and if you had consulted it, you

* Vide " The Fortunes of Nigel," vol. iii., ad finem.

would, I think, have avoided some of the errors into which you have fallen : for instance, from it you might have learned that the first " serious alteration" in the constitution of the Scotch Courts was made in 1724, in that first Utopian period during which you imagine that the " *claymore's edge*" kept innovation at a distance, viz., the Act which prohibited the future nomination of extra-ordinary Lords of Session. The author of the essay does not state who the propounder of the measure was, but I can inform you that it was Mr. Duncan Forbes,—*clarum et venerabile nomen* —one of those eminent men on whom Scotland may justly pride herself.

The next serious alteration appears to have been in that *second* Utopian period of yours, immediately following the American war, when, Sir Walter Scott tells us, that—not an *English-man*—not a young *State Surgeon*—but Sir Ilay Campbell, a Scotchman—a Scotch lawyer—nay, Lord Advocate, and finally Lord President, of Scotland, introduced an important measure of this nature ; and Sir Walter proceeds to inform us, that a few years after (all within the same Utopian period) Lord Swinton, not merely a

Scotchman, but a Scotch Judge, made " in a work of great learning and uncommon merit," several of these very proposals, whose adoption Sir Walter seems to recommend, but of which you, on the other hand, highly disapprove. I trust I may be forgiven if, on such a subject, I agree with Sir Walter Scott rather than with Malachi Malagrowther.

These proposals of Sir Ilay Campbell and Lord Swinton, appear to have been the foundation of the measures for improving the Scotch Courts proposed by the Whig Administration in 1807. I grieve at being obliged to confess, that these measures were proposed by an *Englishman* —not, however a *young State Surgeon* as you apprehend, but, by Lord Grenville, then *Prime Minister*, who probably thought, that in dedicating his great station and valuable time to the conduct of these measures, he was paying a due respect to the importance of the subject, and the feelings of the Scottish people. But, although Lord Grenville introduced them, is it possible that you can be ignorant that they were suggested, prepared, discussed, and approved, by the Scotch part of the Administration; and

that, although there was a considerable difference of opinion in Scotland on the subject, it *was*
a division of opinion, and that if it was opposed
by Scotchmen, it was by Scotchmen also that it
was suggested and advocated ?

What followed ?—When the present Administration, (for I agree with you, that the Administration of to-day may be looked upon as essentially the same,) succeeded the Whigs, that they
found all parties in Scotland were agreed that,
after what had passed, something must be done.

For this purpose two Commissions have been
successively appointed to inquire into the possible improvement of the Scottish law. You
would hardly, I suppose, have had these great
and intricate questions decided without some pre
vious inquiry ; yet, in the bitterness of your wrath
against the Ministers, you complain, like Queen
Catherine, that

————————There have been *Commissions*
Sent down amongst them which have flawed the heart
Of all their *loyalties.*

I had never before heard that this Commission
was unpopular in Scotland, and I cannot but

think, the *loyalty* which could be shaken, as
yours seems to have been, by such a measure,
was, like your plaids, loosely worn, and easily
cast off. In fact, I believe that the principles
on which the first Commission was framed, and
the spirit with which it was actuated, were perfectly satisfactory to Scotland in general. I know
that it included some of the most venerable
names in your country; and the report (besides
the great ability, moderation, and judgment,
with which it was drawn up) has also, in my
eyes, another pledge that it contained nothing
injurious to the feelings, or detrimental to the interest of Scotland, viz., that it was compiled by
the hand, and attested by the signature of *Sir
Walter Scott ;* whom the Commissioners (with
the very reverse of the spirit you impute to them)
had appointed Clerk of the Commission. So
much for the first assault on your National Institutions.

Of the second Commission, you say that it
was composed, " (if Scotchmen *must needs be*
" employed) of those who had been too long
" estranged from the study of Scottish law to re-

" tain any accurate recollection of the abstruse
" science, or any decided partiality for its tech-
" nical forms." And you further intimate, with
corresponding indignation, that " the opinions
" of the Scotch *Lawyers*, nay, of the Scotch
" *Judges*, have been something too much ne-
" glected and controuled in the course of these
" important changes, in which methinks they
" ought to have had a primary voice."

This, as regards the *matter of fact*, is rather an
unlucky series of assertion. I have shewn you that
we have Sir Walter Scott's evidence of the propriety of the constitution and proceedings of the
first Commission. Now let us see whether we have
not even stronger evidence of the propriety of the
second—the Commissioners named in which were
the Lord President, the Lord Justice Clerk, the
Lord Chief Baron, Lord Pitmilly, Lord Gillies,
and Mr. Baron Hume, all *Scotch Judges* of the
greatest reputation and talents ; to whom were
added the Lord Advocate, the Solicitor-General,
and Mr. Cranstoun, three eminent *Scotch lawyers*,
the Professor of *Scotch Law* in the University of
Edinburgh, and the Deputy-Keeper of the Signet

in Scotland; and, further, (in number sufficient to supply information, but not to sway decisions), two English Masters in Chancery, and two eminent English Barristers.

How this roll of names accords with your statement of the neglect shewn in these proceedings to *Scotch Lawyers and Judges*, you must explain— I cannot.

I am not ignorant that few Sessions of Parliament have passed without some attempts at further innovation; and, perhaps, I as little like the spirit of such innovation as you do : but who have been the innovators ? A pack of giddy young Englishmen, as you would have us believe? Whether the gentlemen be giddy or young I will not venture to pronounce ; but as to being *Englishmen*— which is the real *gravamen* of your charge—they are undoubtedly, every mother's soul of them, as genuine Scots as Malachi Malagrowther himself. Mr. Kennedy, Mr. Maxwell, Mr. Abercromby, Mr. Peter Grant, Sir Ronald Fergusson, and Lord Archibald Hamilton, have been the stirrers or supporters of most of those questions; and by whom have they been opposed? Undoubtedly by many respectable Scotch Members, but most powerfully by the English Ministers. If, as you seem to complain, a new Scotch Jury Bill was, after much difficulty and discussion, passed, what were the facts as to that Bill? It was introduced in what was thought an imperfect and injurious form, by a *Scotch* lawyer in the House of Commons, and supported by all that call themselves Scotch Patriots; and it was so pertinaciously pressed that, to prevent mischief, the Scottish Members of the Government were obliged to take it into their own hands, and it was finally carried through the Lords by the Lord Privy Seal of Scotland, and through the Lower House by your Lord Advocate; so that, whether the Bill be good or bad (on which point Mr. M'Wheeble, our hereditary factor at Tally Voelan, has not yet made up his mind), it is evident, Cousin Malachi, that you have to thank or blame your own countrymen for it. What then, I ask, is the pretence for the outcry and clamour which you make, and, what is worse, which you endeavour to spread, that Scotland is maltreated and degraded into "a kind of experimental farm," upon which every *English* quack is encouraged to practise his theories?

I have shown, out of your own mouth, that whatever changes have been made are beneficial; that the quackery of experimentalists has been successfully resisted, and that in all cases the opinions and feelings of the Scottish nation, represented by the Scottish gentry, have been, not merely consulted, but deferred to; and I think I may conclude in the dictum of our relative, Lord Keeper Ashton (as reported in 2nd Tales of my Landlord, p. 25) " That these mutations are *no new sights* in Scotland, and had been witnessed long before the time of this satirical author."

I now proceed to your next grievance.

The Boards of Excise and Customs in Ireland and Scotland have been, it seems, amalgamated with the respective English Boards, and Imperial departments have been thus created for the management of the Imperial Revenue. This to Scotland, is, in your opinion, not only an *injury* but an *insult*. The Malagrowthers are, I readily believe, more sensitive to points of honour, than practised in managing revenues, and your little mistakes upon this head are, therefore, the less surprising. Your national prejudices, and per-

haps some distant prospect of a Commissioner-
ship for yourself, your son, or some of your cou-
sins (on the Malagrowther side), prevent, it
seems, your discovering any other cause for this
arrangement, than that the Irish Board was abolished for malpractices, and that the Scotch
Board was abolished for " the sake of *uniformity*,
to keep them company;" and you illustrate this
by a facetious anecdote of Lord Strathmore's
bailiff, who, having put a malefactor into a pair
of stocks, that stood at one side of a formal court-
yard in the castle of Glammis, hired an innocent
Sawney to fill, for *uniformity's sake*, another pair
of stocks, which had been (also for uniformity)
placed on the other side of the said yard.

The story is a pleasant one, and not the less
amusing for being nothing to the purpose.

In the first place, I deny that the change in the
administration of the Revenue was made on account of *misconduct* in the provincial Boards. It
was framed on a general principle, that as the
Revenue to be collected was, as the French used
to say, *one and indivisible*, it ought, in all reason,
to be managed by *one undivided* department; and

as one Board of Treasury had the supreme con-
troul and direction of the whole, it was alike
absurd and inconvenient that its powers should
be exercised, or, I should rather say, *perverted*,
by three different and often conflicting systems
of administration.

As you have a taste for old stories, and seem
to like them, as one does cheese or game, not
the worse for being a little *stale*, I shall venture
to conform myself to your taste, by suggesting,
that your idea of having, besides a great Board
in London, to manage the imperial revenue, a
little Board in Scotland to manage the Scottish
modicum, is like that of the over-considerate gentleman who provided a large hole for the passage
of his great cat, and a small hole for the accommodation of his little cat! Even Mr. Malagrowther himself will, I think, confess that it is not
likely to conduce either to convenience or economy, to have three holes in the Treasury door.

But if I admit, that in the course of the inves-
tigation which preceded this arrangement, some
irregularities in the Irish revenue were detected,
I am sorry to be obliged to add, that abuses at

least as serious had been, not very long before, discovered in Scotland. Are you ignorant, my cynical Cousin, that in the year 1809 three Members of one of your Scotch Boards were removed for official impropriety? I do not know to what extent either the Scotch or the Irish officers were blamable; I only state the fact, to disprove the whole of your reasoning on this point, and to show, that if the bailiff of Lord Strathmore had been the justiciar of these delinquents, he would, in the first instance, have had to put *your own countrymen in the stocks*, and to have kept them there a pretty long while before Ireland had furnished *her* quota to the *uniformity* of the Castle of Glammis.

I am very sorry to observe that you do not confine your misrepresentation of this point to mere jocularity. You state that Scotland was included in this arrangement, because the Government *durst* not attempt it on Ireland alone. The Irish, it seems, wished for a companion in their misery; and "this gratification of his humours was gained," you say, " by Pat's being *up with the pike* and shillelah on any and no occasion."

This, Malachi, I take leave to say, is sharper

than even " *the edge of the claymore.*" The claymore has been in its sheath for near a century. It
is little more than 20 years since the Irish pike
was red with rebellion and massacre. It is barely
as many months since it has been dyed in mid-
night assassination. Good God! Cousin, what
were you thinking of, when you allowed your pen,
or even your mind, to wander into such perilous
pleasantries—but, after all your fun and your
fury, what is the real amount of the change
either in Ireland or Scotland? Why, no more
than this—Instead of separate and independent
Provincial Boards, standing Committees of the
Imperial Board are resident in Dublin and Edinburgh, who do more business than of old, and at
half the expense.

The ports of Glasgow, Belfast, and Liverpool,
are within twenty-four hours' sail of each other—
they trade in the same articles—they collect revenues for one common Exchequer—yet in each
the business was conducted on systems wholly
different in principle and in practice. Baillie
Jarvie complained, even in his day, of the
Custom-house officers, " who went about on the

" quay, plaguing folk about permits and dockits,
" and all that *vexatious* trade*," and I can scarcely
think that any of his descendants (one of whom
I hear, represents a neighbouring district of
Burghs in Parliament) will agree with you in
thinking that the *dignity* of Scotland requires
that Commerce should be taxed to the amount of
12,000*l.* per annum, for the high privilege of
being puzzled by *three* codes of laws, embar-
rassed by *three* systems of regulations, and
plagued by *three* tribes of officers ; when that
very treaty of Union (of which you happen to
be so strangely and so unfortunately ignorant)
provides especially, that " all laws concerning
regulations of trade, customs, and excise, shall be,
after the Union, the same in England and Scotland." One, indeed, can only wonder, that in
the teeth of the law and common sense such
anomalies should have been tolerated so long.

In the same spirit in which you lament over
the impaired *dignity* of Scotland, in being obliged
to content herself with *three* Commissioners of
Excise instead of *five,* you cast some " longing,

* Rob Roy, vol. ii., p. 273.

lingering looks" towards certain other convenient retreats, in which the *dignity* of Scotland loved to nestle her unfledged offspring, but which the hand of that *durus arator*—the economical reformer—has despoiled:—

> "——at illa
> Flet noctem, saxoque sedens miserabile carmen
> Integrat, et mæstis late loca quæstibus implet."

You are too well read in the erudite tomes of Mr. Josephus Miller, not to know that I have authority for this allusion to a Caledonian nightingale. A Scotch gentleman having heard it asserted that these birds were not to be found beyond the Tweed, assured the company that this was an error, for that he himself had often sen the *nocturnal songster* which he described as being about the size of a small goose, having little red eyes, and a hooked beak, and delighting to sing all night out of an old ivy bush, *whoo, whoo, whoo!*

The Scottish Philomel is, we find, the *bird of Wisdom;* and truly it is in a very prudential and calculating strain that she bewails her devastated nests.

" We have consented with submission, if *not*
" with cheerfulness, to reductions and abolitions
" of public offices required for the good of the
" state at large, but which must affect materially
" the *condition* and even the *respectability* of our
" *overburdened aristocracy*."

Indeed, Cousin, I may say with honest *Stephano*, " You are in your fit now, and your talk
" is not after the wisest ;" for I fancy you will
not meet much countenance in this comfortable
theory of yours, that public employments are instituted for the advantage, not of the public, but of
the happy individuals capable of filling them, and
that it is of no consequence what sums may be
drawn from the pockets of the people, provided
the *kith* and *kin* of the Malagrowthers are gratified and accommodated by a due share of the
sum total.

Your notion of the *real utility* of a public office, reminds me of a circumstance which took
place a few years ago in the House of Commons.

A worthy Scottish gentleman, well known to
you and me, was one evening endeavouring to
move the compassion of the House with a lamen-

tation very similar to yours, over the abolition of a certain class of offices in Scotland, and amongst others, of *one* which he thought it almost treason and impiety to have abolished: " *abolished,*" exclaimed the late Mr. Whitbread, " so far from this office being *abolished,* I apprehend it is actually filled at this moment with great credit to himself, and advantage to the public, by the honourable complainant himself." " A'weel!" rejoined the Caledonian, nothing disconcerted, " a'weel! I'll nae wrangle wi' ye aboot the office itself, but, I say, the auld salary is aboleeshed, and that's far waur!"

But my letter grows too long, and I must, therefore, break off here, and postpone for a day or two, the observations which I have to make on the other topics of your pamphlet. *En attendant,*

I remain, dear Malachi,
your affectionate Kinsman,
E. BRADWARDINE WAVERLEY.

LETTER II.

———

My Dear Cousin,

I shall now proceed to consider what I take to be the chief object, as it certainly was the immediate motive, of your publication; I mean the intention of the Government to endeavour to introduce a metallic currency in lieu of the small notes which now circulate in Scotland to the exclusion of all gold coin.

You profess to have no skill in the *theories* of currency and credit, and you beg leave to consider the question in a purely *practical* view. I pretend to as little proficiency in that most abstruse science, and am as willing as you can be to consider it as a *practical* question; but I fear that we differ as to the meaning of the word *practical;* I think I can see that by a *practical* view, you really mean a view *narrowed* to the present and momentary state of things, and excluding all considerations of what has passed elsewhere, and of what may, at any future moment, occur in Scotland itself; and this I take to be the great error of those who call themselves *practical* men. They confine their observations to the *local spot*, and the *present* day. He who thinks of *to-morrow* they call a *theorist ;* if he looks to the next month, he is a *speculatist ;* but if he attempts to legislate for a year or two in advance, he is deemed a perfect *visionary ;* or, perhaps—the most injurious term the wit of the *practicals* can devise—even a *philosopher !*

But to proceed to our discussion—

I fear that in the very first line of your observations on this part of your subject you have fallen into a mishap, one of the most unlucky which could occur to a *practical* man—namely, a complete mistake as to the *matter of fact* on which you propose to lecture, which is, as you state it :—

" The business of extending to Scotland the

" provisions of the Bill, prohibiting the issue
" of notes under 5*l.* in *six months after the regu-*
" *lation shall be adopted in England.*"

And in a subsequent passage, you imply,
that the effect on Scotland was *at first* intended
to be *immediate.*

" Lord Lauderdale," you say, " almost
" alone interfered, and, to his infinite honour,
" procured a *delay of six months* in the extension
" of this Act—a sort of reprieve from the
" Southern *jougs.*"

Where you have found all these propositions,
or any thing like them, I cannot guess. I live
nearer to the seat of Government, and I never
heard—never read of them. No human being,
to my knowledge, except Malachi Malagrowther, has ever mentioned *six,* or any number of months. Lord Lauderdale's *infinite honour* must, therefore, stand on some other pe-
destal. The most that I can learn that his
Lordship did, was to give to Lord Liverpool an
opportunity of removing some of these misap-
prehensions, which, as the progress of truth is
slow, were, I see, still in full force in Scot-

land at the date of your letter. The sum of what I can discover to have been said was, that measures would be brought forward here-after for Ireland and Scotland, with *such limits as to time*, as the *very different* positions of these countries from that of England might seem to require.

On this false scent, however, you run the rest of your course ; but, at the conclusion of your letter, I find, to my utter surprise, the following postscript :—

" Since writing these hasty thoughts, I hear " it reported that we are to have an extension " of our precarious reprive, and that our *six* " *months* are to be extended to *six years*."

This postscript so alters the state of the case ;—so answers all the charges of *hasty* re-solutions, *violent* changes, and *precipitate* attempts at assimilation, that I only wonder that, instead of adding such an explanation, you did not throw the letter itself into the fire, or that, at least, you did not imitate the candour of the writer of the story of my grandfather " *Wa-verley*," who honestly entitles the last chapter of his work, " *A Postscript which should have been a Preface*."

I have heard of a worthy Highland Gentleman, who, having a favourite servant dangerously ill, sat down to write to the surgeon of the next town to desire his immediate attendance ; but as the Laird was no very expert penman, the poor patient happened to die during the concoction of the epistle. This event, of course, so changed the state of the case, that our intelligent friend thought right to add a postscript to say " Donald is dead, and you need not come ;" and with this well considered missive, a messenger was dispatched to the Doctor's residence, which luckily happened not to be above twenty miles off.

But, without dwelling further on the erroneous statement of your letter, and the inaccurate explanation of the postscript, let us suppose, as is I believe the fact, that the Government never for a moment contemplated any change with regard to Scotland, either *immediate*, or *within six months*, but merely expressed an opinion that some such measure as that which is to come into effect in England in three years, may be advantageous to Scotland at the end of six or seven. What then becomes of your favourite quotation of " *experimentum in corpore vili*," when it is clear that the *experiment* is to be first made upon honest John Bull himself, and that the operation is not even to be commenced in Scotland until it shall have been fully tried and absolutely completed in England !

I am a little at a loss how to correct the misinformation upon which this part of your letter is founded.

I hope you will not be angry if I say, that the errors into which your informant (whoever he is) has led you are so numerous and complicated, that it were tedious to mention all, and difficult to select the principal. Indeed, I may say with *Rosalind*—" There are none principal, they are all like one another as halfpence are—every one fault seeming monstrous till its fellow comes to match it ;" but, I shall endeavour to satisfy you, or at least our readers, as to a few of them.

And first, let me observe upon your indignation, that there should be *any legislation at all* on the subject of Scottish bank-notes—a monstrous intermeddling with Caledonian concerns, which never could have occurred to any man's mind except our State quacks, who would force Scotland to swallow this bitter pill, merely because it happens to be necessary for England.

Again, my dear Malachi, I must give you the trouble, and I fear the pain, of turning to the statute-book, where, I have no doubt, you will be astonished to find, that, in the very heart of the good old times,—viz. in the year 1765,—an Act of Parliament was passed, making the most important changes in the whole paper currency of Scotland, and even destroying " at one fell swoop," the greater part of the circulation, viz. all Bank-notes under twenty shillings, which, I have heard my grandfather say, was, at the time, the only circulating medium in Scotland. This calamitous extermination— this massacre of the little innocents—broke, as our family tradition runs, poor old Mac Wheeble's heart—he never looked up, good man, after the loss of these paper shillings, although there were those who pretended to think that eighty years which had past over his head, and the quantity of Luckie Maclearie's Usquebaugh, which, during the whole period he had poured into it, might account for his decease on less patriotic principles. It is certain, however, that our worthy Baillie deeply lamented the change. He would expatiate by the hour on the advantages of an *exclusive paper currency* —he would ask, what else but the plenty of the *wee-bit* notes enabled the Laird's tenants to pay their rents, and the shopkeepers of Tully Veolan to drive their little trade? As to *silver*, he said it was an expensive article for a poor country to deal in—that he had heard tell that the Southrons had shillings and sixpences of that over-precious metal, nay, even *siller groats, and twal'pennies. They* might, for ought he knew, be able to afford such costly luxuries, but it would be the ruin of poor old Scotland, and he would add, significantly, that the silver dirk of 65 would be found more fatal than the iron blades of the woeful 45. [Indeed, I ought to say that the marriage of my grandmother, and the birth of my father, had a little counterbalanced in Mr. M'Wheeble's mind the other consequences of the latter celebrated year.]

I cannot discover among M'Wheeble's reasons any one which you might not equally apply to the alteration now proposed, nor in your's any which would not have suited his case. But I allude to *this act* more particularly at present, for the purpose of observing, that *it* is the *first* legislative interference which I can discover with the paper currency of any of the three parts of the United Kingdom; so that Scotland, instead of complaining that she is to be dragged at the tail of England, was really the first to introduce these innovations; and it seems that there was no *English* interest to prompt this Bill, for it was introduced by the Lord Advocate Miller, and five other Scottish Gentlemen of weight and consideration, at the instance, and on the recommendation, of some of the principal Scotch Bankers, who had themselves at that time begun to discover (as perhaps their successors will do bye and bye,) that the circulation was in an unhealthy state.

You ask whether " you *argue* your cause too " high in supposing that the intended legisla- " tive enactment is as inapplicable to Scotland, " as a pair of elaborate knee-buckles would " be to the dress of a kilted Highlander." Allow me to reply, that I do not see any very *high* rate of *argument* in this knee-buckle illus- tration, but such as it is, I answer it, by refer- ing to the Act of 1765, and by suggesting that the *gold* knee-buckles offered by Lord Liver- pool are a great deal more valuable, and not less applicable, than the *silver* knee-buckles which constituted the donation of Lord Advo- cate Miller.

This Act of 1765, with many subsequent Acts, which I need not detail, affords a com- plete answer to all that part of your letter which insists that the intended alteration is *contrary to law*, and a direct infringement of the Treaty of Union. But I have a word or two more to say to you upon the manner in which you quote the article of Union on this point.

You tell us that you never saw that docu- ment, and that you have learned the article in

question from the recitation of your grandfather.
I shall show you, I think, that the poor old
gentleman, notwithstanding his pretensions to
accuracy, had a very treacherous memory. The
Article of Union, *as you quote it,* is as follows:
—" That the laws in use within the kingdom
" of Scotland do, after the Union, remain in
" the same force as before, but alterable by the
" Parliament of Great Britain, with this differ-
" ence between the laws concerning *public*
" right, policy, and civil government, and those
" which concern *private* right; that the *former*
" may be made the *same* throughout the whole
" United Kingdom, but that no alteration be
" made in laws which concern private right,
" *excepting for the evident utility of the subjects*
" *within Scotland."*

Let us for a moment suppose that your
grandfather quoted the article in question fairly;
still, I do not see how it can be made available
to your argument. Is it possible that you can
pretend to argue, that a Bill to regulate the
currency of Scotland, and to assimilate it, in
due time, with that of the rest of the United

Kingdom, does NOT concern PUBLIC RIGHT, PUBLIC POLICY, nor CIVIL GOVERNMENT ; but that, on the contrary, this great affair, which you hold to be of such *general, vital, and national,* importance, is merely a matter of PRIVATE *right!*

You have certainly fallen into this absurdity; and it is so manifest a one, that I do not think any further observation of mine necessary to persuade you out of it ; but I have a more serious charge to make against you, or your grandfather, namely, that you have between you, been guilty of a very extraordinary error, in regard to this same article of the Treaty of Union.

It would, I think, be well for the credit of your grandfather's *memory,* if, indeed, the Treaty of Union were as little known to others as it is to you; and I think you will be surprised to hear, that, while the old gentleman affected, with such pretensions to accuracy, to recite the 18th article, he (God knows why,) suppressed the first, the leading and most important, sentence of the article, namely, *that the laws concerning regulation of* TRADE, CUSTOMS, *and* EXCISE,

be the SAME *in Scotland, from and after the Union,
as in England.*

Now, as nine-tenths of your pamphlet are employed in asserting the folly and even the *ille-
gality* of assimilation in matters connected with
trade, customs, and *excise,* it is exceedingly unlucky that these words, which stand in *the very
front* of the article, should have so unaccount-
ably slipped the old gentleman's memory. If
you had been apprised of them, it is clear that
your letter never would have been penned ; and,
I dare say, so extraordinary a suppression will
remind you of the celebrated one of that candid
reasoner, who attempted to prove from Scripture, " *that there was no God,*" by *only* suppressing the first words of the sentence, " *The
fool sayeth in his heart.*"

As I have been so fortunate as to discover
the act of 1765, and to supply the *hiatus* which
your " poor old grandfather " made in the Treaty
of Union, I am satisfied that you must agree
with me, that I have swept away all the objections (which, in ignorance of those enactments,)
you raised to the *legality* of the proposed
measures.

I shall now proceed to explain what I consider the unsoundness of most of your objections to the *policy* and *expediency* of an assimilation of the Scottish and English currency.

And first, let me again revert to the Treaty of Union, the 16th article of which enacts, that " the *coin* shall be the same throughout the United Kingdom," and another article provides, " that a public equivalent shall be made for any " losses which private persons may sustain by " *reducing* the coin of Scotland to the standard " and value of the coin of England."

These provisions prove, beyond all question, that the framers of the Union admitted and established, both in *law* and *policy*, the *principle of assimilation*, and we have seen, that when, in process of time, a deviation from a similarity of currency took place in Scotland, the Imperial Parliament of 1765 stepped in to remove the most prominent difference.

And on *general* principles, I hardly think that even you will deny that this was good policy ; but you say, that Scotland stands in circumstances so peculiar, as to exempt her from the rules which ought to govern all the rest of the world.

You appeal, with absolute confidence, to the prosperity of Scotland, which has grown up under the facilities of *credit*, supplied by the unlimited issues of the paper of the numerous Scottish Banks.

> These reasons (quoth the Knight), I grant
> Are something more significant;
> And yet, they're far from satisfactory,
> T' establish and *keep up your factory*.

I have no doubt whatsoever, indeed, I have personal experience, of the increased and increasing prosperity of Scotland, and I admit that the paper currency may have afforded the capital by which much of this good has been operated; but can any one doubt, that, during the suspension of cash payments in *England* and *Ireland*, advances in prosperity, similar in their nature, though different, perhaps, in their degree, have been made by these countries respectively.

Such a system is specious, and even splendid, but is it *solid?* In England, we think *not*— nay, we think that experience has *proved* that it is not ; and, although it was urged with sufficient pertinacity, and, indeed, not denied in principle, that our gigantic exertions in war, accompanied by such an enormous advance in domestic industry and visible wealth, could not have been achieved without the elastic assistance of a paper currency, yet it has been thought right, and with an almost universal approbation, to return—even at considerable expense and inconvenience—to a metallic circulation in England.

I know not whether an account of the catastrophe of that architectural wonder, the tower of Fonthill Abbey, has reached you. I think it a not unapt illustration of the effects of a *mere* paper system. Nothing was more splendid, nothing could look more solid ; it had stood many winters, and had weathered tremendous gales ; it wore the character, too, of antiquity, and allied itself harmoniously with the lower and more solid parts of the domestic residence ; but, *mole ruit suâ,* and in one night, in weather of no unusual violence, the wonder of Wiltshire was levelled to the dust.

We, in England, have (I hope in good time), seen the danger of this extravagant overbuilding, and we are anxious to exchange for the *solidity* of a metallic foundation, the airy and precarious pinnacles into which a paper currency had enabled us to raise our commercial fabric.

I confess that I cannot see any real, or essential difference between England and Scotland on this point.   You, I know, will say, that the Scotch Banks are *all solid,* while the English private Banks are less to be relied upon ; but, supposing your opinion of the English provincial Banks were correct, surely the solidity of your Scotch Banks cannot be put in competition with that of the *Bank of England ;* and yet it was against the notes of the *Bank of England,* that the Bullion Report, and all the measures which followed it, were specifically directed.

But we now approach the main practical point of the case.

Are your Scotch Banks in reality so solid ? This is a delicate question, and one which, I am sorry, that you, and those who agree with you, have stirred, and stirred with so much pretension, as to make it a necessary ingredient in even the most cursory consideration which can be given to the subject.

I shall deal with it as tenderly as I can. I begin by admitting—and that is as much as I suppose can be asked of me—that the Banks, and the individuals which compose them, are *abundantly opulent*, and possessed, *in the aggregate*, of property sufficient to answer all the engagements they may make. I further admit, that such a foundation is quite solid and sufficient for the general business of trade, and for all the higher transactions of commercial intercourse; but on the other hand, I would ask, what defence do they afford against an *unreasonable* panic, which in matters of paper currency, is the evil most likely to occur, and most necessary to be guarded against? In the late panic in London, firms, possessed—not merely of lands and hereditaments, and such-like inconvertible property, which you represent as being the most satisfactory foundation of the credit of the Scotch Banks—Firms, I say, possessed of *Stock* and *Exchequer Bills* to more than the amount of their engagements, were unable to convert them into cash for immediate use.

You say that only two or three Scottish Banks have failed in a long series of years. I admit the fact, and might say something of the apologue of the *pitcher and the well*, but I think I can, without the aid of allegory, explain the causes, and consequently, the precariousness, of their exemption from accidents of that nature.

The first cause of their uninterrupted credit is, no doubt, their positive wealth, and the great stake which the partners visibly have in the country ; but this cause, as we have just seen in England, is not conclusive against a *panic*.

Sors *hodierna* mihi, *cras* erit illa tua !

The second, I take to be, that the Scotch Banks *hold together*—that, conscious that not one of them could stand, what is called in England a *run*, they help one another for the sake of what is a *common cause*. When a run takes place on a

Bank in Scotland—how is it met? By paying
their notes in *specie?* If that were the case,
you might well boast of the stability of the
Scotch Banks. But I fancy that no such thing
as a payment in coin was ever heard of. The
threatened Bank glorifies itself if it is able to
pay its notes by the notes of one of its neighbours, and thus, by a mutual interchange of support, two Banks, which were objects of suspicion in their respective districts, might weather
the panic by the help of the notes of each other;
and if their proximity should happen to throw
any disfavour on this operation, they need only
have recourse to some more distant corre-
spondent, whose paper should happen to be in
full credit.

This, as I conclude from facts supplied by
yourself, is the real cause that there has been
no loss by the failure of any Scottish Banks.
In the case of the East Lothian Bank, which
seems to have failed, and of another provincial
Bank, which was " *in the predicament of suspicion,*" you say, that other respectable houses

" took up and paid all their current engage-
" ments, *without check to the circulation* of their
" notes, or inconvenience to rich or poor;" and,
proud of these " modern instances," you ask,
" what must be the stability of a *system of credit*
" of which such an universal earthquake could
" not displace or shake even the slightest indi-
" vidual portion ?"

I answer, my dear Cousin, that what you
describe is not a system of *credit,* but of *neces-*
sity on the part of the public, and of *mutual in-*
surance on the part of the bankers. Can that
be a healthy system of paper circulation which
is not even *checked* by the *actual failure* of the
issuers ? Can that be a healthy system, when
other bankers find it necessary *for their own*
sakes (I suppose such acts are never voluntary
or gratuitous) to assume, in a moment of great
alarm and peril to themselves, the engagements
of a neighbouring *bankrupt ?*

Thus the very facts on which you rest your
opinion of the stability of your system, convince me, " that there is something *rotten* in the
state of " Scotland ; unless, in addition to all the

good qualities which you, no doubt, justly ascribe to Scottish bankers, you are prepared to add the hitherto-unheard-of generosity of being just as willing to pay the debts of other people as their own.

As long as this confidence exists, and the public is satisfied with this kind of joint-stock security—as long as the ice continues strong enough to bear you—all is well, and your operations glide along with smoothness and rapidity. But if an unlucky accident should happen; if one or two should fall in, is it possible to calculate how many they might drag after them, or what numbers might perish in their attempt to save the original sufferers?

And who can pretend to say *when*, or *whence*, a general panic may be excited? such a panic, I mean, as should affect any considerable quantity of the paper circulation, and occasion a serious run on several of those banks *at once ;* and who, still wiser, can foretel what the disastrous consequences of such a panic might be?

The holder of the larger notes would probably have no apprehension as to their *ultimate* payment; and he might be able or willing to await the convenience of the bankers, or the conversion of their landed properties into cash; but all the ordinary operations of life, which are provided for by the one-pound notes, would be suddenly arrested—Buying and selling, in all the details which support 'human society, and even existence, would be suspended—the great mass of the people, whose wealth is solely composed of one-pound notes, would be reduced to *sudden beggary ;*—thirst and hunger cannot wait the slow process of a *sequestration ;* —and it would require the pen of the GREAT UNKNOWN himself, to picture the scenes of starvation, turbulence, and misery, which might, nay, which must, ensue during such a crisis.

To say that such an appalling catastrophe is within the verge of *possibility,* is to prove that it is the duty of a wise Government to take precautionary measures against it. No Government can—and no wise Government will attempt to—regulate matters of commercial credit and confidence between parties capable of judging of their own interests, and of making a voluntary option as to the degree of confidence they will give. But, with a circulation *exclusively* of paper, and composed of such very minute parts as notes of twenty shillings, the mass of the people accept them *from necessity, and not from confidence.* What is *credit* in the higher classes, is mere *credulity* in the lower, and that credulity which for years may have given currency to a small note circulation, may in a *few hours* overturn it.

These considerations, founded on general and immutable principles, have, I suppose, induced the Government to interfere with the small note circulation of England, and they apply, in my opinion, with equal force to Scotland.

The mode in which the Scotch banks have established this monopoly, and the way in which it operates, under the specious title of *cash credits*, upon which you dilate with so much complacency, are worthy of a little further explanation.

What is called a *cash credit* in Scotland (like *lucus à non lucendo ;* because there is *no cash* to be seen in any part of the transaction) is managed in the following way :—

A merchant, shopkeeper, or tradesman, goes to a banking-house with two sureties, who become answerable to the bank for his engagements to them ; upon which the bank gives him a credit in their books to a certain amount, according to their opinions of the solvency of the *borrower* (for such he is), and the sufficiency of his bondsmen. Upon this credit the tradesman draws on the banker, who pays the draft by the issue of *his own notes,* and for all his advances charges the borrower with the legal interest of five per cent.; or, in other words, the Scotch bankers receive five per cent. for a handful of paper, which it does not cost them a farthing to create, and for the future payments of which, in specie, they need be at no expense in making provision.

This explanation will also account, in a great measure, for the *unanimity* with which, you tell us, *all* Scotland opposes the intended alteration. I dare say all the bankers (who are in number about 1200), and all the persons whom they *accommodate* with this kind of loan, will oppose any change; but I appeal to every man who has any clear or just ideas of commercial credit, whether a SYSTEM OF ACCOMMODATION BILLS (for that is the right name), which is considered unsound and discreditable in every other country in the world, can be safe and honourable in Scotland.

It is evident, from the foregoing explanation, that the most effective checks which operate to prevent the *over issue* of an English local Bank, are all wanting in the case of a Scotch one. The notes are issued without value in the first instance—they may be forced into circulation to any amount the Banker pleases, for he never, I suppose, can want borrowers—they are kept in circulation as long as possible, for the sake of the interest—and when, finally, the fragility of the material forbids its further circulation and it comes back to the Bank, it turns out to be your *true Phœnix*, which arises again from its own ashes, and takes a new flight as bold and as extensive as its *lately deceased self*. But take care that the day may not come when

you may hear from a hungry populace the same
importunities with which one of the too liberal
lenders of antiquity was visited—

> Immediate are my needs ; and my relief
> Must not be toss'd and turn'd to me in *notes*,
> But find supply immediate. I do fear,
> When every *feather sticks in its own wing*,
> Lord Timon will be left a naked gull,
> Who *flashes* now a *Phœnix*.

I repeat, that I myself have no doubt of the
ultimate security of the Banks of Scotland in
general. I apply my observations, as the Government, I presume, intends to apply its remedy, to those " *depositaries of panic*," the One
Pound Notes, and " the giddy multitude."

Perhaps the Bankers may think that even
these observations of mine may be dangerous.
I might, in reply, administer to them the ter-
rific consolation which Garrick addressed to
Goldsmith, on seeing the latter discomposed by
some slight criticism on a scene in one of his
plays.   " Pooh, pooh, man ! How can you
" mind a squib, who have been sitting all this
" while on a barrel of gunpowder." The object, I believe, of the Government, and cer-

tainly my own, in taking a part in the discussion, is to remove, with due care and circumspection, and with as little danger as possible, the materials which might cause so tremendous an explosion.

This leads me to another, and by no means unimportant, consideration. You argue this question, as if it was *exclusively a Scottish* one, in which England has no *direct interest*, and can only be guided by the silly vanity of extending her own system into the Sister Country; and you illustrate our conduct by that of a crazy Scottish Laird, who was in the habit of forcing one of Anderson's pills down the throat of every guest who visited at his house.

I must confess that, however I may have complained of the unfairness of any of your arguments, I cannot but applaud the *candour* and national impartiality of your jokes; for every illustration which you have given of our English errors has been the recital of some Scottish absurdity.

But admitting, for a moment, that England had no direct interest in the welfare of Scot-

land, would it not be a more accurate illustration, *if we needs must have a medical one,* to com-
pare us—not to a cracked-brained humourist,
who would cram his physic down the throats of
those over whom he has no authority, or guardianship,—but to a prudent parent, who, having
successfully vaccinated one of his children, is
anxious also to place the others beyond the
risk of infection.

But I say, that England, besides her general
duty to the other parts of the empire, *has* a
direct interest in this matter. You forget that
the Picts-wall no longer exists, and that if you
set fire to your stubble, the flames will soon
invade ours ; and, to return to Garrick's metaphor, that you cannot explode a barrel of
gunpowder without doing so near a neighbour
almost as much injury as yourself.

One of your arguments, why England should
not interfere with your concerns, is, I admit, a
strong one, but unluckily, it happens, I think,
to be strong, *just the other way.* The circulation of the Scottish Bank notes is, you say,
" free and unlimited—they pass without a

" shadow of objection through the whole limits
" of Scotland, and are current nearly as far as
" York in England." I am so candid as to be
willing to help this argument a little further ;
for, on my return from Scotland, in last autumn,
I found that the Scottish notes were accepted,
at least, one hundred miles South of York. But,
since this is the case, and since Scottish notes
form some considerable part of the circulation
of the Northern counties, I take leave to ask,
with additional confidence, has England not a
clear *right*—nay, is she not bound by an imperative *duty* towards *her own subjects,* to take care
that they are not made the victims of Scottish
inroads which, though not so bloody, might be
much more extensively calamitous, than the
border invasions of the freebooters of old ?

This objection may seem, at first sight, to be
a slight, or at least, a local one ; but on consideration, I think you will find it to be of immense *practical* importance. I suppose you
will readily admit that if we prohibit the circulation of all English small notes, even those
of the Bank of England itself, we cannot allow

the existence within England of the small notes
of Scotch Bankers; and by what means, if permitted in Scotland, are they to be excluded
from Northumberland? Are we to rebuild the
Pictish wall, and have a Custom-house at every
gate?—or are we to make *highly penal* the
passing a note on one side of an imaginary
boundary, which we sanction as *highly advantageous* on the other? Pray look a little into the
practical details of this part of the subject, and
let us see whether any other mode could be
devised of preventing endless confusion and
difficulties, than that which, in the spirit of the
Act of Union, our Ministers intend to propose, namely, " that the coin and currency of
England and Scotland should be the same,"
and that " the regulations which affect trade
and commercial credit should be assimilated
throughout the United Kingdom."

I now conclude. I persuade myself that
there is so much reason in what I have said,
that you will not—that you *can* not, on a cool
reconsideration, essentially differ from my
general conclusions, and I hope that I have not

been betrayed, either by the tone of peevish-
ness, which here and there marks your letter,
or by the warmth of my own argument, into
any expression inconsistent with a feeling dear
to my heart—the respect and affection, which I
entertain for that admirable, and, (though his
descendant, I will venture to add,) illustrious
person, to whom we are both indebted for our
names and existence.

I am,
Dear Malachi,
Your affectionate Cousin,
E. Bradwardine Waverley.

POSTSCRIPT.

I have just seen your *second* and your *third* letters, but as they add nothing new to the *principles* of the questions which we have discussed, and as it is a tedious, and generally fruitless, labour, to argue about *details,* I am not, in my present temper, inclined to make any observations upon them. If what I have said in these two letters of mine be well founded, your subsequent epistles are, in their main points, answered by anticipation; and if I have not already been successful in making some impression on your mind, I fear the case is hopeless, and that your conversion is not to be operated by consanguineous persuasion.

E. B. W.

LONDON:
PRINTED BY WILLIAM CLOWES,
Northumberland-court.